ROCKETT ST GEORGE
EXTRAORDINARY
interiors

ROCKETT ST GEORGE
EXTRAORDINARY
interiors

Happy Valentine's Day, Darling! Sorry about this book. All the designs are hideous. Apart from the one at p.165. But at least will know what to avoid. I LOVE YOU !!
[signed] xxx

Show-stopping looks
for beautiful rooms

JANE ROCKETT
LUCY ST GEORGE

Photography by **Debi Treloar**

RYLAND PETERS & SMALL
LONDON • NEW YORK

Senior designer Toni Kay · **Senior commissioning editor** Annabel Morgan
Location research Jess Walton · **Production manager** Gordana Simakovic
Art director Leslie Harrington · **Editorial director** Julia Charles
Publisher Cindy Richards

First published in 2017 by
Ryland Peters & Small
20–21 Jockey's Fields,
London WC1R 4BW
and
341 East 116th Street
New York, NY 10029

www.rylandpeters.com

ISBN 978-1-84975-869-7

A CIP record for this book is available
from the British Library.

Library of Congress CIP data has been applied for.

Printed and bound in China

INTRODUCTION

We founded Rockett St George in 2007 but first met years before that at a fancy dress party in the late 1990s. Lucy was dressed in over-the-knee white boots, a white mini dress and wig (a sexy fairy), while Jane was wearing a red sequinned dress, a blond wig and a sash reading 'Miss Leading'. It was love at first sight, and our friendship was sealed when we discovered our shared passion for black clothes, flea markets, Manchego cheese, travel, Tom Hardy and (of course) interiors.

After spending hours trailing around antique fairs and flea markets, rearranging our furniture at home and generally driving our partners and children mad by continually redecorating, we realized that it might be a good idea to join forces and make a career out of our passion. We combined our savings, bought a *Websites for Dummies* book, and Rockett St George was born.

Ten years down the line, we are still best friends and still love a good car boot sale but we have also learnt a huge amount about how to create show-stopping interiors. In this book, we share our decorating mistakes along with our triumphs, we guide you through tricky decision making, and offer top tips on how to achieve magical, surprising and inviting homes.

We have made this book personal with the goal of motivating you to be adventurous and plan properly so you can achieve an interior that dreams are made of. In between each chapter, you will find interior inspiration from beautifully photographed houses and apartments owned by our friends and colleagues, as well as our own homes.

We hope you enjoy this book and that it provides the inspiration for your own decorating journey. Make it personal, be brave, style one step at a time, and enjoy every minute!

IT'S ALL ABOUT YOU   1

LEFT AND RIGHT By keeping the walls dark and understated and covering walls and shelves with quirky accessories and striking art, Cowboy Kate has created a sense of continuity throughout her Cumbrian home without detracting from the unique personality of each room. Mounted antlers, lush greenery and statement artwork are recurring motifs.

MAKE IT *Personal*

There is nothing we enjoy more than poring over interiors books, glossy magazines, Pinterest, Instagram and so on, and admiring gorgeous heart-stopping interiors in a hundred different styles. In fact, this is how the two of us first became such good friends, sharing a passion for interior design, treasure hunting, musicians and vodka (we'll come onto the treasure hunting, musicians and vodka later... well, maybe not the musicians and vodka bit). Never before has there been a time when consumers have had such easy accessibility to home decor products and interiors inspiration. We can indulge ourselves with all the beautiful colours, furniture, art, antiques and textiles that we adore, and are able to access an infinite number of exciting images at just the click of a button.

DECISIONS, DECISIONS

With so many fabulous options available to us nowadays, choice can be a bit of a challenge. Even a visit to the local supermarket is fraught with decision-making as we are bombarded with hundreds of different brands and packaging, all designed to appeal to us. There is even the choice of which supermarket to visit before you have left the house! It sounds great, but too many alternatives can actually be a hindrance as it makes reaching decisions difficult and time-consuming. And when it comes to making choices about how to decorate our home, we all want to get it right first time round.

Some people spend hours deliberating over colours, styles and textures while others find it easy to reach a resolution. Regardless of which category you fall into, we believe that making decorative choices should be fun; a pleasurable process that fulfils your creative needs and leads to a satisfying conclusion. The result should be a home that creates a sense of well-being and rooms that makes you smile every time you walk through the door. This, my friends, is why 'Make it Personal' is the first chapter in this book. Get things wrong and you could spend a long time regretting your decorating decisions.

Indeed, Jane once had her entire bedroom wallpapered at great expense only to arrive home and absolutely hate the result. The wallpaper was patterned, colourful and gorgeous, but Jane didn't feel comfortable in the room. In fact, she felt irritated and edgy; exactly how you don't want to feel in your place of rest. If only Jane had asked herself a few simple questions, she could have avoided making an expensive mistake. In fact, she ended up having to pay to have the whole room done again.

We now know exactly where she went wrong. Jane rushed her decision, listened to other people's opinions and was influenced by a trend that was splashed all over magazines and blogs at the time. Although she loved the design she had picked, she didn't take into account her personal style, the way she used her bedroom, or the atmosphere that she was hoping to create.

If Jane had analyzed her personal style and the ways in which she spends time in her room before making her choice, it would have been obvious where the whole thing was heading. Here's what she should have focused on:

- *She loves a calm, gentle environment*
- *She doesn't wear colour or bold pattern*
- *She likes a rock 'n' roll twist, whether it be zips on her clothes, stars on her jacket or snakeskin on her boots.*

In summary, you could say that Jane is drawn to a clean, tailored look with a dash of punk thrown in. Her bedroom is a place she likes to indulge herself – somewhere to escape during the weekend for an hour or two in order to read, relax or grab a sneaky snooze. It was never going to be the right place for high-energy patterns and colours.

The good news is that there was a happy ending. Jane's second choice of a subtle snakeskin wallpaper in natural hues created the tranquil atmosphere that she craved but it has a cool twist that makes her smile. The Moroccan cushions and wedding blanket draped over the bed head provide a gently exotic and modern ethnic feel that's luxurious and calming. So she got there in the end!

We hope our first piece of advice will prevent you from making the same mistake that Jane did. Our objective is to help you understand exactly who you are and the environment that is right for you. Now this may all sound a little bit deep and serious and, to be honest, it is a bit of a process, but we won't be asking you to meditate just yet. What we are suggesting is that you have a good long think about who you are, what makes you happy and how you live your life. We will be encouraging you to ask yourself some questions about your personality and

OPPOSITE In Jane's bedroom, snakeskin wallpaper, a feather Juju hat and a Moroccan wedding blanket draped over the bed head create a laid-back rock-chic vibe that is true to her sense of style. The simple white bedding and neutral throw prevent the room from looking too busy and create a calm, low-key backdrop that contrasts with the unusual wallpaper.

1 Write down five words that describe your personality, e.g. organized, eccentric, energetic, naughty, serious, sporty, thoughtful, musical, quiet, etc.

2 Write down five words that describe the way you dress, e.g. slick, colourful, monochrome, tailored, boho, rock 'n' roll, seductive, suited and booted, etc.

3 Write down five things that make you happy. This could be anything at all, from the obvious things such as spending time with family and friends to more subtle concepts such as particular smells or feeling the sand between your toes.

ROOM FOR CHANGE

Now you have the key words that describe your personality down on paper, it is time to consider the room you wish to decorate. The way we spend time in the various rooms in our homes varies enormously. The atmosphere we want in the kitchen, for instance, will be very different to the aesthetic required in the bedroom. So there are just a couple more questions to answer.

1 Write down five activities that you would like to do in this room (ok, this may be quite hard for the bathroom but give it a go!).

2 Think of five words that describe the way you want to feel in this room. For example, you might want to feel indulgent, relaxed, peaceful and sexy in your bedroom or sociable, organized and cheerful in the kitchen.

unique individual style. Don't worry – there are no wrong answers here, this is not a test. The questions are just a tool to help you analyze your tastes and needs so you can make the right decisions when it comes to designing your home. But remember – you need to be honest with yourself in order to get the home that you really want.

IT'S ALL ABOUT YOU

Find a pen or pencil and a large piece of paper, pour yourself a glass of wine, relax and write down the answers to the following questions. If you share your home with a partner, you should answer the questions together. Although your individual answers may be different, a common ground can be found (you've ended up together, after all, so you must have something in common!). Your aim is to end up with a sheet of paper covered with words that describe your individual interior style.

READY FOR ACTION

So there you have it. A whole page (or more) of words that describe you and your taste and the function of the room that you want to decorate. You can use these words to determine the right decorative style both for your personality and for your lifestyle. The combination of different styles might be surprising, but they will be right for you. They will provide you with a style template for your home and you can combine them with your room results to achieve exactly the right look for each space.

OPPOSITE The decor of Tina B's apartment in Hove, East Sussex, reflects her theatrical spirit, even in the kitchen. The wall shelves are filled with mismatched glassware, kitsch figurines and even the odd piece of religious memorabilia, while the distressed metal table echoes the rusty red of the brick wall.

BELOW Michael Minns' Victorian house in Hull is all about traditional architectural features given an unexpected modern twist. In the sitting room, an embroidered 'Fetch the Valium' artwork stands out against the glossy black wall to create an attention-grabbing feature. If you look closely, you can see the structure and detail of the original Victorian panelling.

RIGHT We really loved this genius lighting idea for a family home. Alexandra and Nicholas Valla brought a playful twist to this modern fitting by placing a wooden bear inside. When the lights are turned on, the bear creates abstract shadows that dance across the walls.

RIGHT In this book, you'll hear us talk a lot about 'style spots', or creating focal points (both big and small) that make a statement. This is a perfect example. On an ornate marble fireplace in the home of Niki Jones in Tunbridge Wells, hot pink candles leap out against an antique gold-framed mirror. The old photograph that is propped up against the mirror adds a touching sentimental detail.

LEFT AND OPPOSITE Jane's kitchen is an eclectic mix of different styles. The clean white walls and ceramic pendant lights create an airy, modern look while the brick wall and resin flooring have a hard-working, industrial vibe that is echoed in the metal cabinets. Dotted here and there are decorative pieces: old chopping boards, fish-shaped water jugs and a vintage clock, all of which strike a playful note.
BELOW These glass wall shelves are a functional space, home to jars of coffee, teas and sugar, but Jane has introduced a sense of humour and personality in the shape of gold animal-topped jars, greenery, a Jo Lee Ceramics Dolly Teapot and a pineapple vase.

A LITTLE BIT *Rock*

Anyone who's familiar with the Rockett St George brand will immediately recognize Jane Rockett's own home in Sussex. A frequent feature on the company's Instagram page, Jane's home is a style inspiration to many. But what is perhaps most striking about her space is that first and foremost it is a family home. Yes, it's full of the eclectic, maverick Rockett St George magic, just as you would expect, but at its heart is a cosy, lived-in family vibe.

Jane bought her home at the very beginning of her Rockett St George journey and this is evident from the minute you walk through the front door. The Victorian townhouse is brimming with vintage and current Rockett St George pieces alongside treasures brought back from Jane's travels and special mementoes collected over the years and displayed in cabinets and on coffee tables and mantelpieces. In fact, you only really need to see the downstairs of Jane's home for an insight into Rockett St George's development over the past ten years.

Split over three storeys, the ground floor of Jane's home encompasses a kitchen, dining area, home office and living room. Upstairs are her two older children's bedrooms, a spare room and a bathroom, while the top floor is home to her youngest's room, a bathroom and the master bedroom, which was opened up to the eaves by Jane and her partner Toby when they moved in.

What is evident throughout is Jane's rejection of playing it safe and adhering to one particular style. Her kitchen combines industrial brick walls with sleek white counters and mid-century lighting. In theory, such a mix should not work, yet in Jane's house it hangs together perfectly, balancing practical functionality with her own distinctive style.

Jane has been careful to preserve the original features of the house, retaining the original sash windows and wooden floors. But what makes the house unique is the extended dining room with its floor-to-ceiling windows overlooking the garden. The space created by the extension/addition offers respite from the outside world. It is a space where Jane and her family can relax and recharge: something that every family home should have.

ABOVE The dining area is the perfect hangout for Jane and her family. She covered a vintage armchair with cowhide and teamed it with curvaceous rattan lounge chairs. The sloping glass skylights allows light to pour in and the geometric wallpaper on the ceiling contrasts beautifully with the velvety grey-green walls.

OPPOSITE The long dining table takes centre stage, creating a peaceful place where Jane and her family can sit and enjoy a meal together. House plants and fresh flowers create the effect of a lush oasis. The ornate glass chandelier adds an understated elegance to the room and casts a gorgeous sparkling light.

LEFT Rather than using a television as the focal point in her sitting room, Jane decided to create a style spot filled with the many treasures and memories she has collected over the years. Her cabinet of curiosities enjoys centre stage and is filled with photos, children's drawings and beautiful pieces that have great sentimental value. The convex mirror hanging above the fireplace reflects light into the room.

OPPOSITE Stripped wooden floors, bay windows and shutters add character to Jane's sitting room and these architectural features are enhanced by the dark charcoal walls. The leather sofas are dressed with sheepskins and cushions that make the room feel snug and welcoming and the glorious grey linen armchair is a statement piece. The accent lighting is kept deliberately dim to enhance the room's sense of warmth and to create a cosy space for the family to relax in.

RIGHT Jane's workspace is positioned to take advantage of the natural light from the dining space. The wall behind is hung with family photographs and favourite artworks — when Jane is lost for inspiration she look ups from her computer screen and allows the images to spark her creativity. The vintage desk is one of her savviest finds as she found it outside her local Citizens Advice Bureau when they were throwing it out. Like everything in Jane's house, it really works!

LEFT Lola, Jane's teenage daughter, has created a stunning style spot above the Victorian fireplace in her room. The four ornate Rockett St George Melo mirrors are hung in an intriguingly asymmetrical arrangement and are dressed up by a hanging dreamcatcher and wooden hand that she pops her jewellery on.

BELOW LEFT Still in Lola's room, sleek black furniture works beautifully with the pale pink walls. Jane accessorized with sheepskins on the floor and dressing table chair, which is extremely popular with the family's puppy, Angel.

BELOW Full of slick, clean lines and monochrome pattern with touches of gold dotted here and there, Jane's bathroom is airy and light. But what we love most is the lack of clutter. All her lotions and potions are neatly packed away in beautiful storage baskets.

OPPOSITE Jane's guest room has gone over to the dark side. With stunning dark blue walls and a blue spread to match, the room has a moody rock 'n' roll vibe. Gold accessories accentuate the dark walls and add glamour to the room. The headboard depicts oriental images that you could lose hours staring at.

CAREFUL *Contrasts*

The personalities and talents of interior designers Alexandra and Nicolas are evident throughout their stunning Mansard-roofed house in Rambouillet, a beautiful French village located about 40 minutes outside Paris. Divided into six apartments in the 1980s and uninhabited for several years before they bought it, the traditional French house had lost much of it its original character. The couple undertook six months of intensive refurbishment work with the aim of bringing spirit and soul back to the building while preserving its architectural heritage and integrating some clever adjustments in order to accommodate modern family life.

The beautiful parquet floors, plaster cornices/crown moldings, elegant staircase and other period features typical of 19th-century architecture unify this dramatic space. Alexandra and Nicolas have combined these imposing traditional features with modern finishes and quirky accessories and the result is a comfortable yet stylish family home that fits them like a glove. The home is made up of three storeys: on the ground floor is a living room, dining room, kitchen and workshop; upstairs are the family bedrooms and bathrooms, and the top floor is dedicated to guest accommodation.

It's not surprising to learn that the creative couple are the owners of their own business – Royal Roulotte, an interior design company. Their talents are key to the company's success and their look combines their design expertise with their love of fine materials, classic art, flea-market finds and handcrafted pieces. The look is translated perfectly into their own home, which is a testament to their interior design talents.

We were particularly charmed by the personal touches that appear throughout this home: the wooden toys that have taken up residence in the dining room lights, the

OPPOSITE The dining room is a carefully calibrated mix of old and new. The original 19th-century fireplace is painted black like the walls, and offers a contrast in both shape and form to the mid-century chairs that surround the eight-seater dining table. Our most favoured pieces here are the wooden children's toys that have been popped into the Favourite Things glass pendant lights by Eno Studio and the crowded bookshelves piled high with well-read books, both of which add interest.

ABOVE The beautifully detailed encaustic tiled floor in the wide hallway is original to the house. The dark matt walls create an intimate, seamless effect while the low lighting and strings of lights draped around the mirrors further intensify the warm, welcoming feeling.

huge pinboard in the 'craft room', and Alexandra's delicate porcelain clay sculptures, which really add magic to the space. The couple have created a home that suits their personalities perfectly – in person, Alexandra and Nicolas are welcoming, engaging and super-cool, just like their home. They clearly love where they live and feel very much at home in their environment: something that is achieved when interior design is perfectly suited to the homeowners.

One feature that we loved at this house was the innovative use of vintage doors. Alexandra and Nicolas have collected them from flea markets and antique fairs over the years and they lean up against the walls in various spots around the house. Not only do they look fantastic but the doors with hooks work brilliantly in the hallway, kitchen and bathrooms to hang towels, clothes and so on.

OPPOSITE A functioning fireplace with a window above is an unusual architectural feature (the flue runs horizontally and then vertically up the side of the house). Nicolas and Alexandra used a simple but effective symmetrical furniture arrangement to draw the eye straight to the heart of this striking sitting room.

ABOVE AND RIGHT The dining room leads to the kitchen, where plenty of natural light spills in through the large windows. The white walls and plaster cornices/crown moldings create an effortless sense of flow between the two rooms. The oak kitchen table (right) has a playful twist in the form of white-painted table legs while the acrylic chairs add a modern element.

OPPOSITE Simple white walls, patterned tiles and pale pink slipper chairs add vintage charm to the sunroom. But it is the whimsical La Volière birdcage lamp that is the real showstopper. Inside the wire cage are tiny feather birds that tie in perfectly with the vintage theme.

BELOW LEFT In the family's home office-cum-creative space, one wall is covered with a wooden pinboard decorated with lists, plans and personal items such as children's drawings and photographs. The luscious pink swivel chair and large oak desk suit the space perfectly.

RIGHT Nicolas and Alexandra took great pains to restore the building's original features such as the heavy panelled doors. This one, labelled 'craft room', leads into the home office space, which has a sink for clearing up after crafting sessions.

BELOW RIGHT We love the way Alexandra and Nicolas' desk is outward-facing rather than pushed up against a wall. By positioning it right in the centre of the room the couple have successfully created a work space that is family friendly and actually makes you want to sit down and get cracking!

LEFT AND BELOW RIGHT Alexandra and Nicolas' master bedroom takes your breath away. Every corner is a style spot and the tactile bedspread and floral rug are a feast for the eyes. What we particularly love about this room is the brilliant storage. The couple have hidden away what they don't want on show in the huge freestanding glass-fronted armoire and display their most treasured accessories in the salvaged glass-topped wooden display cabinet.

BELOW LEFT For the guest bedroom, Nicolas and Alexandra chose three simple metal-framed beds and pushed them together. The wooden floor is covered with an array of cosy sheepskins that feel soft and snug underfoot. What fun for visiting children to enjoy a sleepover in here!

OPPOSITE There is so much that we love about Nicolas and Alexandra's bathroom. The freestanding bathtub with claw feet works beautifully with the high ceilings and the circular curtain rail above the bath completes the vintage look. The detached wooden door leaning against the wall is a quirky yet practical feature: evidence of the talent and creative genius that lie behind the decor.

TAKE INSPIRATION
(FROM EVERYWHERE)

2

DREAM *Big!*

Equipped with the personal profile created in Chapter One, you are now ready to immerse yourself in all the incredible interior inspiration that's available to us nowadays, safe in the knowledge that you have the tools to identify the look that's right for you. In other words... this is the fun part! When it comes to decorating, inspiration can be found anywhere, from an old movie to the colour combination on a piece of wrapping paper (yes, really!). In this chapter, we want to take you by the hand and show you all the wonderful things there are to see, so prepare to revel in beautiful interiors and get drunk on creativity!

BELOW LEFT The Artist Residence hotels are a great place to get inspired – their eclectic interiors mix modern artworks with industrial furniture and traditional architecture. We particularly love this striking piece of art by Charlie Anderson, which makes a bold statement on a bedroom wall.

OPPOSITE Brody House in Budapest is one of the most beautiful hotels we have visited –the building's spectacular original features include high ceilings, parquet flooring and log burners in every room. The designers chose to strip back the walls to the bare plaster and add modern art and furniture, resulting in a unique hotel design.

OUR TOP SOURCES FOR INTERIOR INSPIRATION

TRAVEL

We are incredibly lucky to have to travel for our jobs and there is not a day when we don't feel grateful for that. Having said that, we have always travelled – when money was tight, we would book the cheapest flights, and negotiate the best deals to ensure that our hunger for travel was satiated. Travel for us is the most inspirational activity there is. Being away from day-to-day life gives us time to consider, daydream and send our minds into free fall, which is when our best ideas happen. In fact the idea to launch Rockett St George occurred when we were lying in the sun together ten years ago. Add to this the wonderful feast for the senses that other cultures provide – the colours of the landscape, the architecture, the lushness of nature, the different styles of living – it is just wonderful. Soak it all up, relax and enjoy your surroundings, then choose carefully what you take from the experience and translate it to your interiors.

HOTELS AND RESTAURANTS

Hotels and restaurants employ the most talented and cutting-edge interior designers on the planet. The brief is always to create a unique atmosphere that will appeal to desired customers. As a result, hotels and restaurants are often great places to steal ideas. Visit a few and, if possible, enjoy a meal in the restaurant, a drink at the bar or a coffee in the foyer (more fun than Starbucks, and the coffee is usually better too!). Take note of everything from the flooring and the lighting to the colour schemes, the art and the use of space. Take photos of things you love so you can recreate them in your own home.

Some of our favourite hotels and restaurants:
Dean Street Townhouse, London The walls crammed with stunning artwork are simply a feast for the eyes. The cocktails are delicious too – try an Eastern Standard.

Brody House, Budapest The juxtaposition of the grandeur of the architecture with bare plaster walls, log burners and uber-modern art is breathtaking.

The Ludlow, New York The floors, the floors, the floors... plus the bathrooms (oh, and did we mention the floors?).

Freemans Restaurant, New York A homely environment that's hard to leave (and the food is absolutely delicious).

Mama Shelter, Paris We love interiors designed by the wonderful Philippe Starck, and he has excelled with the Mama Shelter hotels. His sense of humour has resulted in an interior that both surprises and delights. Painting the ceiling black was a stroke of genius!

El Fenn, Marrakech If you love colour, this is the place for you. The interiors are breathtaking – bold colours combined with incredible tiled floors. Add to this amazing art and statement lighting and the result is a magical Moroccan hideaway that you will never want to leave.

Zetter Townhouse, London The bar in this wonderful hotel is packed with incredible Victoriana.

Artist Residences, London, Brighton and Cornwall The art collections here are fabulous and mixed with vintage finds and comfy furniture to create convivial spaces.

Pikes Hotel, Ibiza Pikes is an Ibizan institution, set in sprawling fairytale gardens with an aquamarine pool. Stay in Room 9 – The Rockett St George suite. Think Rock'n'Roll meets kitsch with a seductive tropical twist.

Hotel Amour, Paris Jane fell in love with the restaurant in this wonderful hotel and used it as inspiration for the conservatory-cum-dining room in her own home.

THE WONDERFUL INTERNET

Sadly we don't all have the money to travel the world and visit restaurants and hotels just because we fancy a change of style in the sitting room. The great news is that you do not have to be a Rockefeller to feast on interior inspiration – we are lucky enough to live in an age where we all have an incredible life-changing source of inspiration in our pockets: our smartphones!

Love it or hate it, the internet is here to stay. We love it, not only because it enabled us to fulfil our dreams of having an online store, but also because it provides us with a non-stop supply of inspiration. If a friend mentions an amazing bar, we can check it out in seconds, if a colleague describes a wallpaper design, we can see it immediately. Today's world is accessible to all, and that is a wonderful thing! The obvious places to start are Instagram and Pinterest, but think outside the box. Search for hotels in Mexico, restaurants in Bali and artists' homes in Byron Bay. Have a nose around houses across the world, check out magazine websites, international designers' sites and more. The world is your oyster, so engage in a spot of cyber-travel from the comfort of your sitting room.

INSTAGRAM

Instagram is genius – think of it as a quick fix for the creative mind. Be it art, interiors, travel, fashion or exercise that moves you, there will be new images, ideas and inspiration available on a daily basis. We suggest that you curate a collection of people who inspire you and add to them as you discover more (but beware – Instagram is also a great distraction when you are supposed to be writing a book... or doing any work at all, come to that!).

Instagram is also a good way to share ideas, get feedback from like-minded people, meet interesting creatives and simply marvel at the crazy digital world that's out there. We have discovered so many wonderful places and met so many inspiring people through this great app – we love it. (Full disclosure: we are not being paid to say this!)

Interiors instagrammers we follow:
@cleoscheulderman, @hansblomquist, @blackshorestyle, @greatinteriordesign, @kim_dti, @belenko, @interiormilk, @elledecoration_nl, @somewhereiwouldliketolive, @elledecorationru, @elledecorationuk, @elledecoration_nl, @elledecorationnorge, @livingetcuk, @houzoslo, @silbellacourt, @chairishco, @myrestaurants, @stylist_nina, @rockettstgeorge (shameless self-promotion!)

PINTEREST

We are sure many of you know and love this creative photo-sharing website, but if not here is a quick guide to what it's all about. Pinterest can be used to create mood boards for anything that interests you and it is especially brilliant for interior design. You can follow people, brands and organizations to view their boards or simply create your own. All you need to do is create a profile and you're off. If you are planning an interior design project, Pinterest enables you to search through hundreds of images and collate the ones that take your fancy. Pin your favourite images to your board and refer to it when you are making decisions on tiles, rugs, fittings, lighting, and so on.

BLOGS

Blogs are a great way to keep up to date with trends and glean inspiration. Bloggers post once or twice a week, but you can also seek them out on Instagram and Pinterest.

Some of our favourite blogs include:

2 Lovely Gays, Abigail Ahern, Brit Decor, Lucy Gough Stylist, Dear Designer, Design Hunter, French For Pineapple, Interior Style Hunter, Lobster and Swan, Mad About The House, My Domaine, Sarah Akwisombe, The Frugality

BOOKS, MAGAZINES AND (BEST OF ALL) HISTORY

When you want a digital detox, there is a wealth of beautiful interiors books out there that are a great source of ideas. Interiors magazines are also fabulous for keeping tabs on new products and trends. International interiors magazines are interesting if you can get hold of them. We love Australian *Vogue Living* and *Elle Decoration* from just about any country.

Our favourite magazines include:

Cabana, Elle Deco, Living Etc, Openhouse, Milk Decoration, Vogue Living

Finally, don't forget history. This a great excuse to watch a few period dramas or movies. Enjoy the dark interiors of Victorian dramas, the glamour of the 1920s and the retro style of the 1950s. History shapes our lives, from fashion to the way we live so, of course, it has a huge influence on our interiors as well. We have a lifelong love affair with Victorian-style interiors, and mixed their dark palette with other styles and a sense of humour to create the distinctive Rockett St George look.

So go for it – spend time indulging in the multitude of gorgeous images and ideas available. Enjoy the process, make the most of all the brilliant technology on offer, and then tailor what you love to suit your personal profile.

BELOW Philippe Starck is the designer behind the Mama Shelter hotel in Paris. The ceilings and walls here are mostly painted black, which results in a warm inviting environment. The walls throughout the hotel are covered with chalk graffiti, creating a relaxed, free-spirited and fun atmosphere.

A WAY WITH *Space*

We have followed Shelley Carline on Instagram for some time now, so we knew that her Sheffield home was an *interior extraordinaire* but how, we wondered, had she transformed an undistinguished 1980s property into such a spectacular home ? After visiting it, we concluded that she must be something of a magician. Shelley has a remarkably creative eye, especially when it comes to small spaces, and, thanks to lots of hard work and a sprinkling of magic, she has created a house that perfectly meets her family's needs. As clichéd as it may sound, good things really do come in small packages!

OPPOSITE The kitchen is a melange of textures and pattern that work beautifully together to create a unique and interesting look. Shelley's talented husband built the kitchen exactly to her specification and it features vintage tin tiles, a wood-clad wall, black metro tiles and a stunning encaustic tile floor. We love the personality and sense of humour that runs throughout this home.

RIGHT AND BELOW Shelley is skilled at curating her treasures and displaying them with an unexpected twist. The snug to the side of her kitchen is cosy and inviting – the perfect spot to curl up in an chair and enjoy a glass of wine. We particularly love the gorgeous leather chair positioned in front of the wood burner and were amazed to learn that it started life a completely different colour. Shelley painted it black to achieve the effect she was after.

2017   February

M	T	W	T	F	S	S
		1	2	3	4	5
6	7	8	9	10	11	
13	14	15	16	17	18	
20	21	22	23	4	25	6
27	28					

LEFT AND BELOW

A vintage apothecary's cabinet takes pride of place in Shelley's kitchen. The unique piece is the central focus of the room and looks just as stunning in real life as it does in this picture. We love the juxtaposition of a modern typographic wall calendar with the traditional cabinet. Add to this luscious green plants, a ceramic African figurehead, apothecary jars and a collection of ceramics, and the result is a masterclass in brilliant display. The little abseiling man (below) slowly descending the wall cannot fail to make you smile.

ABOVE AND RIGHT

The sitting room is jam-packed with unusual ethnic pieces. The sofa overflows with texture and pattern in the form of sheepskins and cushions and a giant Beni Ourain rug covers the floor. Statement pieces include the artwork of an African tribesman and a vintage hide stool (Jane has her eye out for one of these now, as she couldn't quite fit it in her suitcase). The picture wall is a feast for the eyes.

OPPOSITE Shelley transformed the entrance hall using concrete effect wallpaper, oversized faux cacti and a show-stopping swinging wicker chair. Not only has she made a great use of the available space but this welcoming arrangement is a design triumph that sets the tone for what is to come.

Shelley moved into her husband's house in 2004 and, in her own words, transformed it from a 1980s time warp into the eclectic treasure trove it is today. The couple are clearly a match made in interiors heaven: Shelley has an amazing eye for design and spatial awareness while her husband possesses remarkable DIY capabilities. Together they have created a unique home full of ingenious features such as wood-clad walls, rustic shutters, a tin-tiled kitchen island, beautiful parquet flooring, and floating wooden shelves over every radiator.

The way Shelley has used space in this compact home is a design triumph. A dining booth has been slotted in beside the front door. The walls are clad in dark stained wood and Shelley has hung statement art on the walls and accessorised the booth with colourful sheepskins to create a cosy eating area. The sitting room leads off the entrance hall and is also bursting with treasures. It is a cosy and inviting space with more cushions and sheepskins piled on a sofa than you would believe is possible.

At the end of a small corridor is the kitchen. Rather than opting for a large table, Shelley decided to use the available space for a cosy snug surrounding a wood-burning stove. The result is homely yet stylish. Upstairs are three bedrooms and a bathroom, all of them featuring wonderful accessories and ingenious design touches that make this home stand out from the crowd.

Shelley has owned a craft shop since 2008, but in 2015 her hobby became her dream job when she opened Hilary & Flo, an interiors and accessories boutique in Sheffield. The store specializes in unique products from independent designers and up-and-coming artists and is well worth a visit. Shelley is also a keen Instagrammer and regularly shares images of her home and new design ideas.

ABOVE The dining booth is a another effective use of space. Next to the entrance hall, this wood-clad booth is the perfect space to entertain. The colour green is a repeated motif in Shelley's home and creates a sense of continuity.

BELOW The carefully curated theme runs through to the spare room, which features vintage tin tiles and a picture wall. Throughout the house small shelves house mementoes, pictures, plants and items of interest.

RIGHT In the master bedroom, a 1970s-style peacock rattan chair and more leafy faux plants continue the tropical feel. The use of green accents throughout Shelley's home add freshness and life to the dark palette.

OPPOSITE White trees silhouetted against an inky blue wall provide a peaceful backdrop for the master bed.

Wall stickers were a firm favourite at Rockett St George when we launched the company ten years ago and we still have a soft spot for them – they can tranform a space and are quick and easy to use. Shelley's bedroom is a great example of how to use stickers to create an eye-catching look.

ABOVE Displaying in threes is a stylist's trick of the trade. These slightly wonky handmade bowls are a beautiful example of how effective it can look and the natural tones of the bowls pop against the dark painted walls.

WALLS AND CEILINGS

3

RIGHT Jane's 16-year-old daughter Lola had strong ideas about the design of her bedroom. She chose a calming nude pink paint for the walls – it is pretty yet stylish, creating the perfect sanctuary where she can relax. Drama was added in the shape of a monochrome Mr Perswall 'Fashion Covers' mural, which harmonizes with the gentle shade on the walls.

WHERE TO *Start?*

Now you are equipped with your personal plan and a wealth of inspiration, it's time to start making decorating decisions. In this chapter, we will guide you through the process of making the most of any room that you want to decorate, assist you with the difficult decision of what to do with your walls, and offer tips and tricks that will make all the difference to the end result.

ABOVE An exposed brick wall is a classic interior option that brings an industrial warehouse feel to a space. Jane and her partner Toby uncovered the bricks in their kitchen themselves.

It was a messy job but they are delighted with the results, especially as the bricks are old and a variety of different colours. Cleaning up afterwards was not as much fun!

ANALYZING YOUR SPACE

Before you make any decisions, it is important to spend some time considering the room you wish to decorate. You are going to have to do some thinking and ask yourself a few more questions (sorry!).

First of all, what is attractive or notable about the room? Are the ceilings high? Does it have amazing windows? Which direction does it face? Is it a light or dark space? Does it have any period features, such as dado rails, cornicing/moldings or a fireplace? Does the room possess a sleek mid-century vibe or Victorian glamour? What do you like about it? And – just as importantly – what don't you like? These are all things to consider.

For starters, we recommend you write down three things that you like about the room and three things that you don't. For example, when Jane first looked round her home she could see that the sitting room needed a huge amount of work. When she took her children to see the house they unanimously declared that they hated it and would never live there, but Jane could see certain aspects of the room (and in fact the whole house) that could be transformed into something really special.

Things Jane liked about her sitting room:

- *Gorgeous sash windows*
- *Original wooden floorboards*
- *A strange fireplace featuring wood, brick and plaster (one too many textures there!) but that had potential*

And then the less-than-lovely bits — or shall we say the 'challenges' — that Jane's sitting room presented:

- *Woodchip/Ingrain wallpaper on every wall – and we mean every wall, everywhere, all over – nightmare!*
- *Artex/popcorn textured ceilings...and the Artex didn't stop at the ceiling but covered all the cornices/crown moldings as well – yuck!*
- *Ugly curtains covering the gorgeous windows and dirty old carpet on the floor*

By making this list, Jane clarified what was special about the room and was able to identify its potential. It is all too easy to charge into a house and rip everything out, but be careful — sometimes this can remove all the character too, so tread carefully, only remove what you really do not like and make sure you retain original architectural details and personality. Sometimes it is possible to miss things that should be kept. Having said that, if there really isn't anything you like at all, please don't worry. We give you permission to go crazy, tear it all up and throw it all out, then start completely afresh.

Now you have a list of what you want to save, it is time to get busy, remove anything you don't like, and prepare a blank canvas in preparation for getting creative. This work might be as minor as filling a few holes in the walls or as major as stripping wallpaper, pulling down walls or having ceilings replastered (and if this is you, we feel your pain!).

RIGHT Jane painted her courtyard dark grey and used black bricks to construct the barbecue/wood storage area. The result is bold and modern and fits perfectly with the rest of her home. Next on her shopping list is a pizza oven... but do they come in black?

RIGHT Wood-clad walls are a feature of many of the houses in this book. Cladding is a really effective way of adding texture and warmth to a room and creating a rustic theme. If you are a little nervous about banging holes in your walls you could start by hanging a wood-effect wallpaper, which will achieve a similar effect but without the use of a hammer.

LEFT Jane's dining room features glass skylights and dark grey-green walls. She has chosen to wallpaper the ceiling with Smink Things' stunning tile design wallpaper After Lowry. It is a great example of a *trompe l'oeil* wallpaper that really fools the eye, as many visitors ask if it was difficult to tile the ceiling! As well as being a great talking point, it looks absolutely beautiful.

WALLS OF WONDER

We love white rooms with beautiful monochrome accessories – they are stylish, calm and timeless. But nothing gets us more excited than gorgeous dark walls. These are not a modern trend. Historically, dark paints were at their most popular during Victorian times, but they look fabulous in modern, traditional, rustic and urban interiors – they are truly versatile and work well in almost every environment. Once tried, sombre hues are somewhat addictive; they can transform an interior, create instant sophistication, look beautiful day and night and are surprisingly cosy. And, as if this wasn't enough, a lovely dark wall will make all your favourite accessories pop – wood looks gorgeous against a strong backdrop, bright colours sing and plants simply glow.

Choosing wall coverings and colours can be a minefield, as there is so much to consider and mistakes can be expensive. The first factor to take into account is the direction your room faces as, believe it or not, light from the north is completely different to that from the south. South-facing rooms are flooded with warm natural light all day long and you can pretty much do what you want with them, whereas a north-facing room will receive a harder, cooler light and can be trickier to decorate.

If your room faces north, our best advice is to opt for a warm-based colour with underlying brown and yellow tones and to avoid cooler, blue-based hues. For example, Lucy has a gorgeous rich black on her bedroom walls, but it has mellow brown undertones that create a cosy effect. A blue or grey-based black would feel less welcoming.

If your room faces east or west, consider when you will spend the most amount of time in there. The light will change dramatically in these rooms throughout the day – east-facing rooms are generally bright and sunny in the morning while west-facing rooms tend to get the best light in the afternoon and early evening. It's important to consider the time of day that you are likely to use the room and the balance between natural light and a colder light when the sun is not in the room.

OPPOSITE BELOW
This has to be our favourite wall in the book. Cowboy Kate painstakingly created the effect by applying gold leaf by hand and the result is breathtaking. The gold adds a warmth and glamour to the room but it also reflects the light, adding life and energy. Both of us are trying to work out where we can recreate this look in our own homes!

ABOVE Michael Minns has carved out an area on his landing to house a home office space. By covering the walls with reclaimed wood he has cleverly zoned the space, separating it from the rest of the stairway and landing. The wood was salvaged from a house in Bali and features peeling paint and different tones and textures.

ABOVE RIGHT The vertical strip of white metro tiles in this downstairs cloakroom accentuates the height of the ceiling and the elegant architecture of the house. The use of a brightly coloured wallpaper is surprising and fun; it adds interest to one of the most essential but overlooked rooms in the house.

RIGHT Children's rooms are made for bold murals or papers and they are the perfect place for getting super-creative. This little girl's bedroom in a Paris apartment is covered in The Wild wallpaper by Bien Fait – a gorgeous monochrome jungle scene featuring animals, birds and tropical plants.

SAMPLE POT MADNESS

All of us have covered our walls in a patchwork of coloured squares and still been none the wiser as to which shade will work best. In our experience, the most reliable way to test a colour is to paint a large piece of lining paper (or old wallpaper) in the shade you want to try, ensuring that you apply at least two coats. Then position the piece of paper in various different parts of the room, attaching it to the wall using low-tack masking tape. The paint will look quite different at different times of day, in lighter and darker areas or with the lights on or off, so you want to make sure it works well in different circumstances. Also try sticking the paper into a corner so that the colour reflects back onto itself, which will change it again.

Choosing the right shade is a tricky game, but by moving the paper around the room you will get a much clearer idea of how the paint will look all over the walls. The final decision is, of course, now down to you!

STICK IT

Wallpaper is another great option for walls. There are so many beautiful papers on the market, from stunning traditional patterns to graphical modern designs, and some interesting textures too. We are big fans of trompe l'oeil designs that mimic tin ceiling tiles or stripped wood. Avoid the feature wall, which can now look dated, and paper the whole room. Remember to apply all your personal style rules to your choice – opt for a design that will suit you and your lifestyle as well as making your heart skip a beat every time you enter the room.

Do not be scared of doing it yourself either. If you are DIY proficient with an eye for detail, wallpapering is not as difficult as you might think. If you are reading a book on interiors, you must be a creative person, so all you need is a bit of time and patience and you'll be fine. There are lots of helpful guides online to get you started. There are also removable 'peel and go' wallpapers and wall stickers on the market now and these are perfect for renters or for anyone who gets bored easily.

DO NOT NEGLECT YOUR CEILINGS!

The ceiling is a much-overlooked surface but – trust us – decorating it is an easy way to provide the wow factor.

PAINT IT

There are two options here: either paint your ceiling the same colours as your walls, which is subtle yet stylish and creates a seamless effect, or choose a contrasting colour. We saw this effect in a traditional-style bathroom with a black floor and white metro tiles. It was a lovely room, but what made it stand out from the crowd is the fact the ceiling was also painted black. It looked fabulous and the room was elevated to another level thanks to a simple coat of paint. We know what you're thinking, but don't worry: dark colours do not make a ceiling feel lower. If anything, they make the ceiling disappear as they create the impression of infinite space above, plus they are a brilliant backdrop for a glamorous light fitting.

WALLPAPER IT

Wallpaper can convert a blank white ceiling into a spectacular decorative statement: Jane has used the beautiful After Lowry wallpaper by Smink Things on the ceiling of her dining area and it has created a real talking point. Another favourite design move is to use a simple geometric design in the kitchen – it looks fabulous.

TIN TILES

Whether you use the real McCoy or the replica wallpaper, tin tiles conjure up New York lofts and a sense of industrial cool. Lucy used them in her home office and not only do they look amazing but they also reflect the light and create the illusion of an even higher ceiling.

So there we are: the starting points sorted. Once you have taken time to get to know your room and, most importantly, its key features, the styling and accessorizing of the rest of the space can begin.

ABOVE In Michael Minns' house in Hull, painting the living room ceiling jet-black was a brave move but it works. Rather than making the ceiling feel lower, the room looks and feels bigger, as the the black fades into the background, creating an increased sense of space. The inky hue also provides the ideal backdrop for a stunning vintage glass light, which might have been lost against white paint.

ABOVE RIGHT Make the most of the smallest room in the house. We think the cloakroom is a great place to go for a bold look and a touch of luxury. In her house, Lucy has covered the sloping ceiling and two walls of her downstairs lavatory with Cole & Son's Piccadilly wallpaper, leaving the walls black for a dramatic contrast.

RIGHT Lucy used tin ceiling tiles in a light metallic finish to make the most of her high ceilings and create a wow factor. The tiles cast a gentle reflective glow from above and add texture and glamour to her home.

SCENE *Stealer*

Situated on a leafy side street in Hull, Michael Minns' home stands out from its neighbours thanks to its black woodwork and striking black front door. Owner of ShootFactory, a successful locations company, Michael bought the house because he wanted a project where he could let loose with his dramatic interior style and – oh my – has he created something special. Michael documented the process of transforming his home on his blog, 47 Park Avenue. He started the transformation by tearing out decades' worth of clutter and chintz to create the perfect blank canvas while ensuring that the property's original Victorian features were left untouched. He then transformed the five-bedroom house into a home that suits him down to the ground.

Michael's style of interior design isn't for the timid or faint hearted. As with most collectors, it has taken him years to collect and display his possessions in a way that satisfies him and the result is truly breathtaking, with each and every room in the house offering a different atmosphere that is both surprising and delightful.

As soon as you walk through Michael's front door, your senses are bombarded with colour, texture and contrast. The hallway leads directly to the front sitting room, which is a dramatic, theatrical space with pure white walls, a

OPPOSITE AND ABOVE RIGHT Michael's living room has bright white walls and flooring plus a black ceiling. This is the perfect backdrop for the unusual modern chandelier (above right), which creates great impact and, teamed with the use of symmetrically hung mirrors and bold artwork, gives the room a modern twist. Michael's unique scheme for this room teams statement pieces with colour blocking to create a living room with a whole lot of wow.

RIGHT In one corner of the room, Michael has created a fabulous style spot using a pair of lovingly restored black vintage chairs, an Eero Aarnio fibreglass table that's to die for and a flourishing fiddle-leaf fig (well, who wouldn't be happy to live in this gorgeous house?). On the tabletop, Michael has curated a selection of items of different heights, including a stack of oversized art books, pieces of sculpture, glass display domes and the most exquisite vintage lamp.

LEFT Dark walls are the perfect backdrop for statement pieces. Here, within a mainly monochrome scheme, Michael's pink velvet sofa explodes against the black walls of his second sitting room. The unexpected colour pop adds sophistication and a sense of fun to the interior. You can almost hear the sofa calling your name, drawing you in, inviting you to take a seat and enjoy the space.

black ceiling and peacock blue accents. Behind this is the second sitting room, which Michael had panelled and painted black before adding a huge statement pink velvet knole sofa from George Smith. In both sitting rooms, vintage glass lights adorn the walls and ceilings, and modern artwork completes the look. The third sitting room is more colourful, with a leather Chesterfield sofa offering a snug corner to relax and enjoy a cup of tea.

On ascending the stairs, we were struck by the clever use of space on the landing, where Michael has carved a neat home office out of a narrow area by the banisters.

OPPOSITE The second sitting room echoes the scheme of the first sitting room, but in reverse. With bold black panelling on the walls and bright white ceiling and floor, this is monochrome heaven. The dark walls make Michael's bold artwork leap off the walls while the vintage Italian glass wall lights and chandelier not only illuminate the room but are a work of art in their own right.

FAR LEFT A glimpse into the third sitting room from the hall. The vibrant yellows, pinks and oranges of the oversized painting give the impression that the sun is shining out of the room. The sleek organic lines of the Arne Jacobsen Egg Chair provide perfect contrast.
LEFT This classic tan Chesterfield sofa provides a warm contrast to the wall, leaving you with just one decision: whether to lounge full length on the Chesterfield or to swivel in the Egg Chair?

ABOVE This is a bedroom that dreams are made of. Two large airy rooms have been knocked into one to make a wonderful suite. The ingenuous idea of using the semicircular sofa as a bed head not only joins the two rooms together but helps to define zones within the space.

ABOVE RIGHT Vintage cabinetry and oversized vases are used to display some of Michael's collections.

RIGHT Why not have a chandelier in the bathroom? We love Michael's fabulous idea of hanging one from metal scaffolding poles – such a framework can be

made to any height and can even be moved from room to room if fitted with castors. Michael has used a vintage display cabinet to showcase more of his treasures along with the practical items that are necessary in all bathrooms, making the ordinary extraordinary.

THIS PAGE Texture, light, rough luxe and glamour are just a few of the words we would use to describe this room. With a pair of matching vintage ceiling lights, an exposed brick wall, vintage display cabinets and a freestanding bathtub, this space is a wonderful example of warehouse chic.

Then (drum roll...) you reach the main bedroom, and this is where Michael has really excelled. He knocked two bedrooms into one, stripped one wall right back to the original brick, plumbed a freestanding roll-top tub into the middle of the room, installed double sinks and suspended a working chandelier from a framework of scaffolding pipes. The end result is a spacious loft-style sleeping and bathing space. Add to this two beautifully designed dressing rooms kitted out with quirky storage, much of it reclaimed, and you have an interior that dreams are made of.

Michael is one of life's true visionaries. He is absolutely fearless when it comes to decorating and doesn't conform to the expected. His use of colour and texture is masterful, his magnificent collection of vintage lighting is an inspiration, and his home is a feast for both the eyes and the senses.

OPPOSITE Bathrooms can have a sterile feel and don't always feel homely. Michael has treated the design of his bathroom just as he would any other room in the house, and the mirrors, furniture and chandelier give the room personality and a glamorous feel. He has preserved all the functions of a bathroom but without the trappings of a conventional design.

THIS PAGE Long has there been a trend for non-fitted kitchens, but the non-fitted bathroom is still a novel choice. If you have the space for one, they can be a spectacular feature. Here Michael opted for a minimalist low-profile shower and a freestanding vintage bathtub.

LEFT The vintage 'The Board Walk' sign is a bold and brilliant feature on the way up to the master bedroom. At the top of the stairs, Michael has created a home office space on the landing and demarcated the area using reclaimed wooden cladding and oversized statement lighting.

BELOW Michael has the luxury of not one but two dressing rooms. This one features an Sputnik-style vintage ceiling light and an covetable collection of art, but our favourite piece here has to be the amazing shoe storage.

OPPOSITE Michael's attention to detail is second to none and nowhere more than in his second dressing room. He had the room tiled and added bold metal type to introduce personality. The vintage cabinet is dressed with giant glass jars and a smiling Buddha. To top it all off, Michael's shoes are displayed in a vintage glass cabinet. Jealous? We are!

ABOVE Metro tiles together with pieces of signage add style and interest to the second dressing room. The monochrome colour scheme is mirrored by the collection of clothes hanging below. Michael does storage really well.

STYLING YOUR SPACE
(A LITTLE BIT AT A TIME)

4

BRING IT *Together*

If all is going well, you should now be in a position to start adding furniture, lighting and accessories to your interior. An empty room can, however, be rather a daunting prospect and it's often difficult to know exactly where to begin. Don't feel overwhelmed – we are here to help! In this chapter, we talk about how to design a room little by little in order to create your dream space.

ABOVE Lucy has created a seating style spot in her kitchen/dining room. The cowhide rug and sheepskins create a warm, comforting vibe while the plants provide a sense of connection to the garden and the faux zebra head adds humour.

We really enjoy chatting with customers about their interior plans and are often asked for advice or pointers on how to go about designing a room. If it doesn't come naturally to you, we have come up with a plan to guide you through the styling process, starting with baby steps and moving on to larger areas. It's all about building confidence, experimenting and being brave enough to just give different things a go.

STYLE SPOTS

In this chapter, you'll hear us talk a lot about 'style spots'. By this, we mean a focal point that grabs the eye. A style spot is a grouping of furniture, artwork and lighting that fits beautifully together and creates impact. When planning a room, we encourage people to split the space up into sections such as the fireplace, the seating area, the entrance and so on, then to consider each one as an individual style spot. This is much easier and less daunting than designing a whole room, and by narrowing your focus and styling a small group of furniture, artwork and lighting you will make a really impactful display. It is possible to design one area at a time – before you know it, the whole room will have been transformed into something wonderful that miraculously all hangs together.

PRACTICAL MATTERS

Before we get too carried away with the entertaining pastime of styling your home, it is important to do a little more practical thinking. You will need to consider exactly how you will use the space you are designing. For example, how many people sit and watch TV here in the evening? This will obviously affect the amount of seating you will need. If you regularly entertain family and friends, you will require a large dining area with perhaps an extendable table. If space is limited, you may need to fit a desk and computer area into your living space. All these factors will affect your design and are very important to take into account if you wish to achieve a practical, flexible room that works for you and your family.

THIS PAGE A feature piece in its own right, here the Rockett St George Wheatsheaf Table is at the centre of a gorgeous little style spot. The coral ornament, lump of crystal and the base of the table offer a fabulous combination of textures and forms while the beautiful blue candleholder has an iridescent gleam in the light pouring from the bay windows.

GO WITH THE FLOW

The flow of your space is very important. Is your room warm and inviting, does it entice you in and tempt you to spend time there? It's always worth shifting the furniture around and trying out different combinations for a week or so to see if a new arrangement works better. When we first met, long before the days of Rockett St George, we shared a passion for interiors and spent hours rearranging our rooms. It is amazing how this can change the energy in a space and create a fresh, positive atmosphere. Why not move your sofa to a different place, or try your bed in a different position? Lucy likes to be able to see the door and the window when she sits in bed, so much so that she enlarged her bedroom window and positioned her bed to allow her a view of Alexandra Palace when she drinks her tea in bed on a Sunday morning.

We know a lot of people struggle with change and you may find the idea of rearranging furniture uncomfortable At first a room that's been moved round can feel slightly 'wrong', but sit with it for a few days and see if you still feel the same way. Go on, try it!

OUR TOP TEN TIPS FOR ARRANGING YOUR SPACE

1 Always maximize natural light – take down heavy curtains and allow the daylight to flood in. **2** Don't automatically push furniture up against the walls – try placing it in the middle of the room, as this gives the illusion of more space. **3** Never arrange your seating area around the TV. **4** It's impossible to overestimate the importance of lighting (and we'll get onto that in the next chapter). **5** Beds should always have a view – if you don't have one, create a style spot to look at (perhaps a dressing table or chaise longue). **6** Ensure that every seat has a view too. There should be a beautiful style spot to please the eye wherever you sit. **7** In the kitchen, take advice from the professionals with regard to layout, space and storage. Then adapt the plans to suit your style. **8** Creative storage – and lots of it – is essential. Think tall kitchen cabinets, beds with drawers beneath and capacious cupboards. How can you have a beautiful interior if you haven't got somewhere to hide all the things you don't want out on display? **9** If you don't love it, upcycle it, swap it or recycle it. **10** Keep mixing it up!

THE RSG STYLE SPOT MASTERCLASS

Although the process of planning a room for maximum functionality is important, what we really want to address in this chapter is how to create interiors that raise eyebrows, make you smile and stand out from the crowd. Styling is the enjoyable, creative and exciting part of interior design... so let's have some fun!

THE COFFEE TABLE
(AKA THE STYLING NURSERY SLOPES)

A firm favourite of Instagrammers everywhere, the humble coffee table is a great place to start honing your styling skills. Here you can create a display featuring a carefully curated selection of items that you love. Focus on

ABOVE Shelves, tabletops and chests of drawers are the perfect spaces for a style spot. Boutique owner Helene Morris has turned this beautiful sideboard into a piece of art, dressing the top with ornaments and artefacts that are a range of different heights, materials, textures and sizes. We particularly love the large circular mirror – it completes the whole look and reflects light into the space.

gathering together objects of different heights and textures to create a journey for the eyes. We recommend coffee-table favourites such as beautiful books, candles and plants to start you off, but it's essential to inject your own personality so make sure that you include items that are precious to you and reflect your taste.

Have fun, change your arrangement around often and exercise your stylist muscles in preparation for larger areas. Don't forget to take a pic and share it using the hashtag #stylespot – everyone loves a 'flat lay'!

SHELF HELP

Another area that is brilliant for your stylist training is shelves, whether they are wall hung or part of a bookcase or cabinet. Each shelf offers an opportunity to create a decorative arrangement, whether it is composed of kitchen accessories, sitting-room ornaments or bathroom lotions and potions. Start by removing all the objects that you no longer find beautiful. If anything has not been used for the past few months, then throw it away. If it's something useful or essential, put it away in a cupboard. We love this part – it always feels great to declutter and curate only the pieces that you really love.

Once you've weeded out the objects that you don't want, you should be left with items that delight your eye. Now you have your curated collection, consider heights, shapes, colours and textures, group like items together, layer your look and always add a quirky surprise. Don't forget to use all the inspiration you have available to you (see chapter 2). Try to recreate scenes that you find on Instagram and let your creativity flow. Then, when you have created your display, go on and take a #shelfie!

THE NEXT STEP...

Once you've honed your styling skills on smaller areas, you are in a position to move on to larger areas such as fireplaces, living-room seating, hallways and bedsides to create your own style spots. Treat each space individually: select pieces of furniture, art, mirrors, lighting and add a few key accessories to complete the space.

OPPOSITE BELOW In their hallway, Alexandra and Nicolas Valla have used a palette of moody, sensuous tones and added a point of contrast in the shape of a colourful table lamp. The natural forms of the coral and shells are echoed in the vintage prints in brass frames that hang on the wall.

ABOVE Helene Morris has made her dining table the focal point of this space. The beaded chandelier is texturally pleasing and casts patterns of light over the table at night. The table centrepiece injects a little greenery into the room and beautifully complements the large bowl vase, while the tall candlesticks lead the eye up to the unusual chandelier above.

THE FIREPLACE

If you are lucky enough to have a fireplace and mantelpiece then it is a great focal point (so much better than the TV) and an excellent place to practice your styling skills. Mirrors always look gorgeous above a fireplace, as do pieces of art. When it comes to styling a mantelpiece, remember our advice – you need a selection of items of different heights to intrigue the eye and it's important to layer objects so they aren't just lined up in a row. Scale is key – lots of small items can end up looking cluttered and insignificant so it's worth sizing up and choosing a couple of larger pieces for impact. Symmetrical arrangements are often effective but equally an asymmetrical mantel can look more modern and 'undecorated'.

THE HOME OFFICE

A home workplace is a wonderful spot to express your creativity as it will give you pleasure every time you sit at your desk. Storage is essential in this kind of space and

offers an opportunity to add visual interest. Wall shelves and vintage-style wire wall units will keep a small desk clear of clutter while a larger desktop allows you to add plants, photos and fun desk accessories plus fantastic stationery (we definitely have a thing about stationery).

THE SOFA

Whether you have a streamlined modular design or a traditional buttoned three-seater, the rules are the same. Dress the sofa with cushions and throws and don't neglect the wall behind. Add a couple of side tables at just the right height to hold books, TV controls, reading lamps and cups of coffee, and arrange plants, art and other favourite accessories to complete the look.

THE OCCASIONAL (OR STATEMENT) CHAIR

This has to be our favourite style spot. A statement or accent chair is a wonderful thing and is a brilliant way to update a room without having to splash out on a new sofa or other big pieces. A rattan peacock chair, a wing chair upholstered in vibrant velvet or a curvy retro design are just some of the options. Just add the right lighting, a fabulous cushion and a side table, and you're done!

THE BED

Another great styling opportunity is the bed. Dress it in layers – add cushions/pillows and chunky throws or sheepskins to create an inviting vision. Don't forget the wall above the bed: options include wall hangings, art, photos and other accessories – Jane has a feathered Juju hat hanging over her headboard. Bedside tables should be functional, i.e. large enough to hold everything you need but also contain some visual treats – a glamorous feature lamp, a trinket tray, a candle and other bits and pieces.

THE DRESSING TABLE

This a great place to show off. Don't be afraid to hang your favourite dress or coat on the wall as a display. Store jewellery on a stand or in glass display boxes, and use art,

postcards and decorative items to create a personal look. Makeup or perfume bottles look good massed together on a mirrored tray. A dressing table is where you transform yourself, so make it special and indulgent.

THE BATHROOM

The best way to style the bathroom is not to think of it as a bathroom but like any other room in the house. If it's a large room, there's no reason why you can't use unfitted furniture – chests of drawers and cabinets – and unconventional storage such as a vintage drinks trolley will create a talking point. If you have a simple modern bathroom, warm it up with wood in the shape of a mirror or towel rail and introduce contrasting textures – baskets for towels, and magazines. And the bathroom is a brilliant place for plants, whether they're faux or the real McCoy.

So go for it. Experiment, take risks and think outside the box, but always bear in mind your personal plan – your home should be all about you and the things you love.

OPPOSITE ABOVE LEFT Lucy's workspace is a beautiful mix of industrial style and minimalism. Her vintage metal desk is complemented by the artwork and plants and the leather chair adds a sense of laid-back comfort to the space.

OPPOSITE ABOVE RIGHT Dark walls are the perfect backdrop for an ornate mirror, quirky lampshade and vase of seasonal foliage The antique desk and chair complete the style spot, while the black leather armchair adds a rock 'n' roll twist.

RIGHT Cowboy Kate's living room is a feast for the eyes. Bursting with sheepskins, ornaments, artworks, books, plants and so much more, you could spend hours examining the many beautiful displays throughout her home. We particularly love the sofa layered in sheepskins, which creates a very cowboy-chic effect.

THIS PAGE The dining room is a decadent feast of Cowboy Kate's trademark sheepskin rugs combined with a huge ornate mirror that instantly draws the eye. We particularly love the large dining table which, with its uneven, rough-hewn edges, adds a charming cowboy character to the room. Dark walls add impact and drama while an intricate antique chandelier illuminates the room and reminds us of a bygone era.

LEFT We both wanted to rush straight home and recreate this stunning paint effect in Kate's dining room! **RIGHT** Expressing Cowboy Kate's brilliant personality, this alcove in the hallway is a fun and imaginative style spot. A white bust makes an eye-catching centrepiece and is playfully dressed in a cowboy hat and bullet belt. The traditional table lamps create a pleasing symmetry while the gold mirror creates an interesting backdrop.

COWGIRL *Chic*

Cowboy Kate first popped up on our radar when we took a virtual tour of her home on Instagram. Her real name is Jane Learmonth, but Lucy called her 'Kate' for half a day before this was revealed! Her Cowboy Kate Insta-handle is a homage to the iconic book *Cowboy Kate and Other Stories* by legendary photographer Sam Haskins, who was renounced for his witty, insouciant and beautifully executed images of women. Interestingly, we think that there is a striking parallel between Haskins' work and Cowboy Kate's beautiful home.

Kate and her husband John live in a 400-year-old house in Cumbria and as soon as we stepped through the front door we knew we were somewhere very special. So much so that we immediately wanted to turn around, head straight home, paint our kitchens, rearrange our furniture and get creative! There is not a single spot in this house that does not bear testament to Cowboy Kate's creative touch. Every room is crammed with art, stunning lighting, leafy plants and cowgirl memorabilia. Throughout the interior, dark tones cloak the walls, yet every room has its own unique character. With such a feast for the eyes we didn't know where to look first and found ourselves walking round in circles saying 'wow' a lot!

The first room we fell in love with was Kate's sitting room, which is home to a variety of different sofas, each one piled high with the sheepkins she sells in her online boutique. The dining room elicited another chorus of wows, thanks to the stunning chandelier hanging low over the dining table, the floor-to-ceiling windows and, last but not least, the exquisite paint treatment on the walls. Kate applied dark paint over light paint, then rubbed on gold leaf in seemingly random places to create the most magical of effects. It seems as if the surface of the walls is peeling

LEFT Geometric tiles provide a brilliant focal point in Cowboy Kate's kitchen and immediately draw your eye to the peacock blue AGA. The room is a mixture of the modern and traditional, and the dog statue standing to attention beside the stove adds an unexpected twist.

BELOW LEFT Rather than hiding it away in cupboards, Cowboy Kate keeps her all-white tableware out on display. Not only does it look great as part of her monochrome scheme, but it's also close to hand. The terracotta wine rack below the shelves contributes another eye-catching geometric pattern to the room.

RIGHT The large airy kitchen has both functionality and style. Unfitted cabinets and drawers offer stylish storage space while the straw hats hanging from the wall by the back door inject a sense of playfulness and the chandelier adds understated glamour.

away to reveal gold hidden beneath. Teamed with giant artwork, African Juju hats and Rockett St George palm tree lights, the overall effect is truly breathtaking.

Although the interior is bold and dramatic, many of the components are simple – the dark palette and repeated use of plants and sheepkins, for example. Upstairs, the dark walls of the hallway are hand-painted with a mural of waving palm trees. The hallway leads to a decadent black and gold bathroom that's adorned with plants, candles, bird cages and a vintage rattan peacock chair.

Just like the rest of the house, the seductive master bedroom has dark walls and features Kate's signature sheepskins as well as a delightful vintage dressing table, and a globe chandelier. There are carved wooden screens

at the windows instead of curtains, and the walls are covered with artworks, fans and photographs.

Kate's home is a masterclass in successful style spots – they are everywhere you look. Each one is balanced perfectly; framing a window, adorning a shelf or covering a table. Take a leaf out of her book and start styling small areas one by one. Before you know where you are, you will have created something truly stunning.

OPPOSITE Kate's style is unashamedly maximalist. She owns a company selling sheepskins and her home is the perfect advertisement for her products. In the sitting room, shaggy fleeces cover the sofa, creating a cosy and welcoming environment.

ABOVE The grand piano takes centre stage here, along with a huge Swiss Cheese plant. Like so much else in Kate's home, the piano stool is draped with sheepskins. The floors have not been neglected – Kate has covered them with zebra hides and stripy rugs.

RIGHT At the other end of the living room, Kate has created a picture wall hung with arresting monochrome artworks by Gill Button. The retro-style table lamp casts a warm, flattering light over the boxy leather sofa, making this the perfect reading spot.

ABOVE LEFT In the sitting room, Cowboy Kate built bookshelves into a wide, arched wall niche. What we found particularly striking about these shelves is that Kate has turned all the books the other way round to hide their multicoloured bindings. It is a quirky idea and ensures that the various book covers don't detract from the dramatic decor.

ABOVE RIGHT The square leather armchairs in Cowboy Kate's living room work really well against the more traditional styling of the mirror, lampshade, desk and chair. We love the white-painted floors that, along with the large floor-to-ceiling windows, really brighten the whole space up. Finally, the pops of greenery placed around the room really breathe life into the space.

RIGHT The shelves behind Cowboy Kate's sheepskin-covered sofa (see previous page) are carefully curated. Filled with an eclectic mix of Siamese cat figurines, antlers, favourite magazines and natural treasures, the shelves are jam-packed with personality. They are illuminated with subtle accent lighting that's in keeping with the low light levels that Cowboy Kate prefers.

OPPOSITE Here a gorgeous gold circular mirror pops against the dark walls and is the first thing to capture the eye. When sticking to a dark palette for walls and furniture, contrasting shapes and textures are important, otherwise everything just merges into one. The leather furniture has a soft, tactile sheen that makes it stand out from the velvety walls.

ABOVE LEFT Cowboy Kate's bedroom is a dark paradise. The bed is layered with blankets and sheepskins for a cosy and calm effect. Hanging above the bed is a bleached bull's skull, which continues the cowboy theme that's prevalent throughout this home.

ABOVE RIGHT This is a thing of beauty – a black rattan peacock chair with an elaborate, intertwining pattern. Dressing the seat is one of Cowboy Kate's signature sheepskins, which transforms the chair into an inviting reading nook.

LEFT Cowboy Kate's master bathroom is a study in dark decadence. Add twinkling candlelight and lots of greenery and the effect is truly magical. Taking centre stage is the freestanding bathtub, which is illuminated by a cluster of candles. An oversized ornate mirror on the wall above the tub enhances the feeling of luxury and indulgence.

OPPOSITE Cowboy Kate's dressing table sits in front of floor-to-ceiling windows that allow natural light to flood in. As in the rest of the house, there is a feeling of luxurious sophistication created by the antique French-style dressing table, upholstered armchair, glass ceiling light and the two-seater sofa. Cowboy Kate has accessorized this space with oversized green plants and special treasures. The effect is spectacular.

LIGHTEN UP

CREATE THE *Mood*

Have you ever been to a restaurant where the food was delicious and the company charming, yet somehow you felt a little uncomfortable and ill at ease even after a glass or two of wine? If the answer is yes, it's likely that the room was brightly lit with high-wattage overhead lighting. This is an incredibly common interior mistake, yet is so easily remedied. The right lighting can make or break a room design but it is very often the last consideration when designing a room.

THIS PAGE The designers of this Parisian apartment suspended five vintage-style glass pendant lights over the kitchen table. The slight blue tint of the glass means the lights harmonize perfectly with the cobalt blue fabric on the bench seating. The lights are fitted with a variety of vintage-style lightbulbs and are controlled by a dimmer switch so the light level can be adjusted to suit any occasion.

BELOW LEFT Lucy chose Tom Dixon's oversized Copper Round Pendant ceiling lights for her sitting rooms. They reflect the light beautifully and look fantastic off or on. The warm, rich copper hue is the perfect foil for her polished wooden floors and deep blue walls.

As far as we are concerned, lighting is the most important factor when it comes to creating an attractive and inviting home environment and there is no part of the decorating process that is more important than selecting the right lights. Of course, lighting primarily has a practical function but when used well it also creates an welcoming atmosphere and helps us to relax. In this chapter, we take a close look at the different types of lighting and how they can be used to enhance a living space.

Mother Nature is a genius when it comes to lighting. Dawn and sunset are perfect examples of how light can influence your mood and enhance your life (as well as your interiors). The morning light is gentle and kind and at the same time fresh and energetic. It inspires us to get moving and embrace the day, but there are shadows and contrast too, which create interest and ambience. Take inspiration from this type of light for spaces where things need to get done – kitchens and home offices, for example.

Our favourite natural light has to be the rich, golden evening light as the sun is setting.

LEFT Michael Minns has sourced many incredible vintage statement lights for his home in Hull and this beautiful chandelier is no exception. It is suspended from the high ceiling of his entrance hall, offering the perfect welcome. We particularly love the way the sparkling metal and glass are silhouetted against the black-painted ceiling.

BELOW LEFT A classic Jieldé articulated arm wall light is the perfect choice for this kitchen in a Parisian apartment. It offers excellent targeted light for food preparation and the matt black finish perfectly matches the monochrome accessories.

BELOW Space is often at a premium on bedside tables as they tend to be piled high with books, magazines and other bits and pieces. This pendant light hung by the bed in Alexandra and Nicolas Valla's home is a great solution to this problem. We particularly like the use of the golden textile flex, which adds colour, personality and warmth.

OPPOSITE Helene and Robin have chosen the Rockett St George Molecular light for their kitchen. The linear design and metal finish blends perfectly with the monochrome scheme. This light is both beautiful and functional – perfect for this stunning space.

Gentle and kind, this light relaxes and calms us as it fades slowly into night and should be imitated in areas where we wish to relax, such as the sitting room and the bedroom.

It is essential to consider all the different activities that will take place in the room you are designing and then to choose the correct style of lighting accordingly (obviously not forgetting to keep your personal style plan at the front of your mind). In some cases, this may differ from occasion to occasion, so make your lighting flexible and always, always fit a dimmer switch.

In this chapter we examine different types of lighting and how to use them to enhance your interior design, and provide some top tips for effective lighting.

LIGHTING TYPES

TASK LIGHTING – FUNCTIONAL YET STYLISH

It is essential to have enough light to work or read by and kitchens, home offices and bathrooms all need effective task lighting. We suggest choosing directional lights that boost illumination in the area required without blanket lighting the whole room. A great example of task lighting is the iconic Anglepoise. This articulated lamp has an elegant, pared-down silhouette and casts a concentrated pocket of light to work by. Pendants are great task lights and work brilliantly when suspended over kitchen islands and worktops. Wall lights are also good for illuminating a work area, especially if you opt for designs that are adjustable and can be angled to cast light exactly where it's wanted.

A reading light has to be effective and again we suggest an articulated lamp for this, especially if you love to curl up in bed with a book. If you have a favourite reading spot, make sure that you factor in a decent lamp when you plan your room design.

STATEMENT LIGHTING – MAKE A SCENE

We do love a statement lamp – they excel at creating impact and are a fantastic interior design trick, stepping your interiors up to the next level. A statement light is

usually oversized and flamboyant, such as a beautiful chandelier or an iconic molecular ceiling light: either way it must be spectacular. If a statement lamp is hung as a central fitting make sure you fit a dimmer switch so that it twinkles and sparkles rather than dazzles and glares.

A statement light looks particularly fabulous over a dining table or in a hallway. Bear in mind that if the light is heavy, you must ensure that it is screwed into a joist to avoid pulling your ceiling down. We would always suggest getting a really good electrician to wire this sort of fitting.

Don't be afraid to install a statement light in an unexpected place. Why not put a chandelier in the kitchen or hang one over the bath (sadly, you definitely won't be able to wire it to the main electricity supply. But who cares? The effect will be stunning – and, as we said, statement lights are not about the light but the fitting.)

CREATIVE LIGHTING (... AND RELAX)

As mentioned earlier, we love the light in the evening as the calming effect of the setting sun casts a warm, flattering glow and atmospheric shadows. To recreate this effect at home, you need to create pools of light and shade. We recommend using table and floor lamps and wall lights to create a cosy, intimate atmosphere, remembering to highlight artwork and illuminate reading areas. This type of creative lighting is perfect for living spaces that are used for relaxation and entertaining.

If space is an issue, opt for wall lights to keep the floor clear. We particularly love it when bedside lights are fitted either side of the bed as in a luxe hotel; this is a great way of providing a lovely and very practical reading light but it also leaves lots of space on bedside tables for all your other bedtime essentials.

String or fairy lights have a wonderfully magical effect, and you are never too old to feel magical, so do not be afraid to use them in your home to sprinkle a little bit of magic: they never fail to make us feel sparkly and festive! We suggest that you hang them over a mirror, drape them over plants or attach them to the wall.

NEON

Neon is more of a statement or perhaps even an artwork than a functional light, but we cannot ignore it in a chapter about lighting. If you want to add a twist to your interior, neon is a winner. You can now also purchase more cost-effective LED neon, which looks just as wonderful. So go on... treat yourself to a little neon wall art!

THE ULTIMATE MOOD ENHANCER – CANDLELIGHT

The absolute daddy when it comes to lighting has to be candlelight. This light is alive, it dances, it glows and, let's face it, it makes us all look just a little bit more beautiful. It will also make your interiors glow, so make it a daily ritual to light your candles to enhance relaxation. We live such hectic lives that it is important to slow down and relax and candlelight enables us to do this.

LEFT String lights are definitely not just for Christmas. We suggest using them to brighten up dark corners, simply hanging them wherever you wish to relax. Switch off your other lamps and let the twinkling lights lift your mood. Lucy has hung delicate trailing flower lights over the mirror in her sitting room and it adds a feminine note to the space.

OUR SIX RULES OF LIGHTING

1 Fit a dimmer on every light you have. They will allow you to adjust the light level of a lighting fixture, changing the atmosphere from businesslike to intimate at the flick of a switch. **2** Do not rely on a single ceiling light to light a room: it will cast a blank, hard overhead light that is a friend to no one. By all means opt for a fabulous ceiling light... just never turn it on! (And if you really have to turn it on, make sure that it has a dimmer switch.) **3** Never install a fluorescent light in any part of your home. **4** Choose your bulbs carefully. Edison-style light bulbs are a style statement in themselves. Avoid cool white LED and go for the new, warmer tones. **5** You can never have too many table and floor lamps. **6** Light candles every day!

THIS PAGE The stylish and functional kitchen in Quentin Leroux's Parisian apartment features black cabinets with white marble worksurfaces and a single floating shelf. The kitchen area is cleverly demarcated by a strip of tiled flooring inserted alongside the traditional parquet flooring that runs throughout the rest of the apartment.

BRING ME *Sunshine*

Designed by renowned design duo Alexandra and Nicolas Valla of Royal Roulotte (see their home on pages 26-33), Quentin Leroux's apartment in a traditional Parisian building is a triumph of both style and function. Without compromising the property's elegant architectural features or Quentin and his family's unique sense of style, Alexandra and Nicolas have created a truly inspiring yet family-friendly living space. The original period detailing of the apartment is still intact and the interior is spacious and light with polished parquet floors, plaster cornices/crown moldings and floor-to-ceiling windows.

Tall glass double doors lead from the hallway into the main living room. Here, the coffee tables and boxy sofas are pared-down mid-century designs that chime perfectly with the understated elegance of the panelled end wall. The adjoining wall is covered with Ellie Cashman's dramatic large-scale Dark Floral

wallpaper and a double doorway at the other end of the room leads to a smaller, more intimate seating area lined with fitted bookshelves painted a rich navy blue. Featuring a mix of dark blues and geometric patterns, the two rooms are linked by bright gold curtains that hang at all the windows and provide a sense of warmth year round. What is perhaps most delightful about this space,

however, is the family's grey cat: it's as if he was chosen because he matched the furniture so perfectly!

The kitchen is spacious and bright with a seamless run of sleek black cabinets along one wall. Opposite is fixed bench seating and a chunky wooden kitchen table plus a mix of mid-century seating. Above the table hang five delicate glass pendant lights that bring additional visual

OPPOSITE ABOVE
The architecture of this light-filled apartment is instantly identifiable as Parisian. The doors, floors, windows and traditional features are all typical of the classically elegant Haussmannian apartments we dream of living in.

OPPOSITE BELOW
Classic furniture and modern lighting and accessories are mixed perfectly in this striking family home.

LEFT The luscious golden curtains that hang at the living room windows are a stroke of genius. The vibrant hue creates the illusion that the sun is shining in, no matter what the weather. This effect, combined with the inviting mid-century sofas, the Tom Dixon Copper Round Pendant Light and the flash of dramatic floral wallpaper, results in a room we would like to hang out in while enjoying a glass of French wine and listening to someone playing the piano.

interest but do not detract from the backdrop of artwork and mirrors propped up against the wall.

The main bedroom embraces the dark side with a twist. The panelled blue walls are teamed with warming touches of gold to create a space redolent with luxury and tranquillity. The headboard is covered with a gold and navy geometric wallpaper and minimalist brass wall lights

cast enough illumination to read by. The white ceiling retains its original cornicing and stands out against the dark walls. The room is accessorized with antique mirrors, a fringed ceiling light, a large fireplace and a guitar propped in the corner. And the gold curtains that feature in the living rooms also appear in the bedroom for a dramatic effect that ties the whole space together.

OPPOSITE Leading off the main sitting room shown on the previous pages is a smaller seating area featuring a deep dark grey linen sofa. This more secluded space would be the perfect place for watching a movie, we thought, and of course that is exactly what this spot is for – the room features a projector and pull-down screen for maximum film fun.
RIGHT Mid-century style chairs are upholstered in a graphic black-and-white print that picks up the pattern of the rug. The custom-made dark-painted shelving and cupboards are the perfect place for the family's library.

OPPOSITE In the bedroom a freestanding wall acts as a bedhead and conceals clothes storage behind. The wall has been papered in a contemporary geometric print that repeats the colour scheme of inky blue and soft white with golden accents.

ABOVE Original features are worth their weight in gold. Here, gorgeous traditional brass door fittings pop against the saturated blue of the door.

ABOVE RIGHT Throughout the apartment, streamlined modern pieces have been teamed with traditional and antique features. In this case, elegant bare bulb light fittings and a floating wooden shelf work perfectly alongside the panelled walls and and an antique mirror.

RIGHT A delicate fringed ceiling light adds softness to the bedroom and is reflected in the oversized mirror above the chimneypiece. Painting the frame of the mirror the same colour as the walls has given it a contemporary twist. Notice how the vibrant golden curtains bring a glow of sunlight into the room.

OVER TO *The dark side*

Deborah Vos is a self-confessed interiors obsessive. A fan of the dark side, Deborah's love affair with interiors started around 15 years ago when she discovered a passion for modern design. This passion soon developed into an obsession, so much so that she has recently taken a career leap and started a venture as an interior stylist. Deborah lives in an Edwardian end-of-terrace house in west London with her husband Tim and their family. As you step into their home you are engulfed by the rich, shadowy hues of Abigail Ahern's Mulberry Red and Madison Grey paint. The effect is one of soothing relaxation that makes you feel instantly at home.

BELOW LEFT Deborah has well and truly gone over to the dark side, painting her walls and ceilings in gorgeous, tactile shades from Abigail Ahern's paint range. Dark walls are the perfect backdrop for artwork and accessories – they make colours pop and statement pieces sing. The darkness is cosy and inviting and, of course, incredibly cool.

OPPOSITE The Ligne Roset black leather Togo sofa is what interior dreams are made of. Deborah has combined it with a 1970s-style pedestal coffee table and string lights to create a really inviting seating area.

Deborah has chosen to enhance the period features of her home with a moody, cocooning colour palette. She knocked two sitting rooms into one, retained the original fireplaces and painted the walls a warm grey shade. One end of this space is bursting with vintage vases picked up at car boot sales and auctions plus myriad faux plants and blooms. The other end of the room features a huge circular mirror, yet more vases and eclectic objects found on Deborah's travels. There is a mix of vintage and high-street furniture, including a leather Ligne Roset Togo sofa that we were lusting after.

The room is also home to a sleek Saarinen-style coffee table and a vintage drinks trolley that Deborah bought on a whim and drove home on her scooter. The walls are hung with art and photographs by Nan Golding plus sketches by Deborah and Tim's talented children, Maddie and Harry. Deborah is a photography graduate and has hung one of her giant artworks in the hall.

Lighting is a key feature in this home and in the sitting room Deborah removed the central ceiling fixtures, opting instead to light

the space with wall lights, table and floor lamps, string lights and candles. Books, artefacts and photos are displayed on custom-built bookshelves and illuminated with small accent lights. The scattered light sources soften the room and create a cosy haven that's difficult to leave.

The dark colour palette extends to the bedrooms, which have a calm, restful vibe. The master bedroom is furnished with vintage metal pieces softened by a vintage chandelier, string lights and Deborah's artworks.

What we love most about this home is that the interiors have lovingly evolved over the 20 years that Deborah and Tim have lived here. Their home has an air of comfort and contentment that only comes with time.

OPPOSITE Deborah's house is brimming with wonderful pieces collected over the years. An ethnic wooden cabinet is piled high with vintage suitcases and the mantelpiece is home to favourite pieces of art. Every spare piece of space is adorned with plants and flowers, vases and ornaments.

ABOVE A deep blue velvet sofa covered in an eclectic mix of cushions sits comfortably beside a floor-to-ceiling bookshelf that Deborah painted the same colour as the walls, creating the perfect backdrop for her treasures and books.

FAR LEFT AND LEFT Deborah loves to fill vases with flowers both real and faux. The green adds a freshness and life to her interiors and her huge vase collection is to be coveted.

LEFT If you are using a limited colour palette, it's so important to introduce different textures to bring interest and depth to your interior. Deborah's sitting room is a brilliant lesson in how to do just this. She has mixed smooth leather with fleecy sheepskins, a shaggy Moroccan-style rug and large mirrors to achieve an eclectic modern look.

ABOVE This dramatic hot orange and yellow artwork really pops against the dark grey walls of the sitting room. Deborah has created a perfect style spot here by combining an angular mid-century leather sofa with the statement artwork and a beautiful contemporary floor light. At the other end of the sofa is a psychedelic purple and white 1970s table lamp that we would rather have liked to take home with us!

BELOW At the far end of the living room, a vintage metal desk and an Eames Soft Pad chair sit beneath the windows. This looks like the perfect place to work, surrounded by interior inspiration and natural light. Plus there is that fabulous 1970s table lamp again – it really is a great vintage piece.

RIGHT The bedroom is all understated luxe, with a stylish padded bed head and sumptuous velvet throw all in the same shade of grey. Deborah has a really good eye for art and she has curated and hung a gorgeous collection of monochrome pieces above her bed. The result is a stylish yet relaxing environment.

OPPOSITE Deborah has added soft feminine accessories in the shape of a vintage chandelier, velvets and sheepskins. These contrast with the shiny finish and right angles of a huge industrial drawer unit. Combining contrasting textures can be hard to get right but it results in the most impactful interiors.

ABOVE An artful juxtaposition of masculine and feminine styles can be seen throughout Deborah's home. In the bedroom, she has combined graphic black-and-white photographs with a gracefully trailing string of tiny lights.

COLLECT, CURATE
AND DISPLAY

6

SHOW OFF IN *Style*

We are often asked how to create a unique interior – one that really stands out from the crowd. Our answer is always the same: you are completely individual in every way, so the secret to creating a unique look is simply to express your own personality in your home. Perhaps the easiest way to achieve this is by displaying carefully curated favourite items in a creative way. Whether it is objects you have made yourself, family pieces, vintage kitchenware or precious children's art, it can all look fabulous when displayed well.

Jane collects items from every country she visits: it might be something as simple as a pebble or as exotic as an ostrich egg. She displays these mementos in a cabinet in her sitting room and they are a constant reminder of happy times. Jane loves telling the stories behind the items in the cabinet (if she can find anyone to listen!). There's even a heart-shaped leaf in there that her daughter gave to her years ago. The display is very personal but it is also an eye-catching decorative feature.

Lucy's house is quirkier. She likes to collect anything that catches her eye or makes her laugh. The shelves in her kitchen contain everything from Coca Cola bottles designed by Jean Paul Gaultier to a Batman mask brought

OPPOSITE Jane's glass-fronted display cabinet is overflowing with items collected over the years that have huge sentimental value – they range from shells collected on the beach in Mozambique to a clay penguin made by her daughter Eden when she was very small. Family snaps are propped up alongside favourite ornaments and her prized piece of vintage coral.

LEFT Lucy's shelves are bursting with personality and irreverent humour. The skulls, collected on her trips to visit her brother in Mexico, are particularly striking.

ABOVE These versatile Rockett St George brass frames can be used to display different-sized images such as playing cards, art postcards and children's drawings.

back from a trip to Paris. The shelves and the collections housed on them tend to change and evolve with the seasons – for example, Lucy adds sequinned reindeer, vintage decorations and framed notes to Father Christmas at Christmas time.

One of our favourite displays belongs to a photographer we know who has collected vintage cameras for years. He shows them off on three floating shelves painted white (the same colour as the walls). The effect is beautiful: the old black and silver cameras stand out against the white background, creating a graphic display that is full of personal significance.

Other great items to show off include album covers, vintage magazines, book covers, handbags, hats, and our favourite – kitchenware! We love kitchenware: ancient bread boards, wooden spoons, beaten-up pans, antique bottles and handmade ceramics can create such an eye-catching feature. And they're so much easier on the eye than blank cupboard doors.

OUR TOP TIP

Always curate (sort the wheat from the chaff) and display your chosen pieces well – remember less is more.

ABOVE LEFT Tina B is the mistress of collecting, curating and displaying and this fabulous collection of brooches is proof of her skilled eye. Her decision to display them on a vintage mannequin is inspired and the result is a eye-catching piece of art.

ABOVE CENTRE Tina's handbag collection is to be admired as much as her impressive display skills. She has used an old fruit-picker's ladder to hang her bags, again creating a piece of art that doubles as storage.

ABOVE RIGHT Haphazardly hung hats make a great talking point in Cowboy Kate's kitchen. The natural tones and textures of these straw hats and the wooden walking sticks stand out beautifully against the dark walls. This is such a great example of how everyday items can be displayed creatively to achieve an eye-catching effect.

OPPOSITE At one end of her kitchen, Lucy's picture wall extends all the way around the corner into the seating area. The black-and-white themed pictures blend perfectly with her monochrome dining furniture and the faux taxidermy zebra head.

AUCTION

The Prettiest Star!

THE PICTURE WALL

Anyone who follows us on Instagram will already know that we are slightly obsessed with picture (or gallery) walls. In our opinion, there is no better way to let your creativity run wild. Although art can be expensive, creating your own picture wall need not break the bank; you just have to think outside the box a little. You can frame pretty much anything – images from books, old letters, postcards, album covers, a baby's t-shirt, photographs of family and friends, a favourite necklace, children's drawings, and so on. Items of different shapes and sizes are essential – you will need a few larger pictures to 'anchor' the arrangement.

Frames Opt for a variety of different frames rather than sticking rigidly to one colour or finish. This looks more interesting and friendly and gives you the freedom to add different frames as your collection grows.

Design Before hanging anything, lay out your frames on the floor to devise a layout and make sure that they work well together. Start with your favourite (or largest) image in the middle at eye level, then build outwards from there. Try to create a story or arrange items that share a common look or subject together. You could go for a classic grid configuration, or think outside the box and go vertical (Pinterest or Instagram are great for picture wall inspiration). Add a dash of humour and personality by including unexpected items such as faux animal heads, framed notes or other personal items. Anything that makes you smile.

Grab a friend Some jobs are best done with a buddy. Once you've decided on the positioning of each picture, be accurate and measure out exactly where you want your pictures to hang on the wall. Space artworks at least 4 cm/1½ inches apart to give each one room to breathe. And always use a ruler and spirit level for best results – nobody likes a wonky picture!

THIS PAGE Helene's kitchen is a striking combination of dark cabinets, clean white walls, white worksurfaces and a gorgeous curated collection of kitchenware. She and Robin chose slate grey for the cabinets and the white floating shelf against the white wall creates a feeling of space that would have been lost if they had gone for wall units. Being keen cooks, the couple spend a lot of time in their kitchen and every item has been carefully chosen for its functionality as well as its beauty.

PERFECT *Flow*

Helene Morris's home is one of those interiors that makes you want to rush straight home and redecorate your entire house. There isn't an item here that hasn't been carefully considered and simply everything is beautiful and stylish – even Helene's rubber gloves are chic! As the owner of Neilson, a beautifully curated fashion boutique in Cuckfield, West Sussex, Helene has exquisite taste, and this is evident in her inspired decorative choices.

LEFT A vintage shelving unit offers stylish storage for Helene and Robin's kitchen accessories. A iron Japanese-style teapot, white ceramic jugs, a white stovetop coffee maker, storage jars and potted herbs all combine to make a pleasing display.
RIGHT Even Helene and Robin's knife collection looks like a piece of art alongside well-used chopping boards and other utensils.

Helene and her partner Robin live in a Victorian semi-detached house that boasts high ceilings, large sash windows, skirting/base boards to die for and numerous other fabulous architectural features. The couple stripped the floors and painted the whole house in a gentle, subdued shade of white, choosing a neutral palette of blacks, greys, warm browns and metallics for the interior. Every room is full of carefully collated treasures, mixing antique fair finds with modern artwork and unusual finds. The result is that the whole house flows gently from room to room and there's something of interest on every wall, shelf or surface: it is a feast for the eyes!

Upon entering the large hallway vistors are greeted by Helene and Robin's lively Jack Russell terriers, Margot and Elvis, who, perhaps unsurprisingly, match the colour scheme perfectly. The front sitting room is dominated by a large shuttered bay window and furnished with deep leather sofas and cosy throws and rugs, providing the perfect place for the couple to relax with their two teenage children, George and Claudia, and the dogs.

The kitchen is at the back of the house and is reached via the dining room. Monochrome is the theme here, with statement lighting, black-painted fireplaces and vintage shelving. What makes this room so appealing is that it is real. Nothing is for show. All the beautiful items here have a purpose: the stack of breadboards is used on a regular basis, the candles are lit each and every day and the piles of cookbooks are well thumbed.

Upstairs are three bedrooms, a dressing room and a bathroom. The master bedroom is simple and peaceful, featuring tactile natural materials and stars on the wall above the bed.

Helene is a skilled stylist and every room features carefully curated style spots. We particularly love her use of traditional art in the kitchen, the chandeliers in the bathroom and the unique lights that adorn every room (all of which are on a dimmer).

But perhaps the most wonderful feature of this home is something that cannot be shown on the pages of this book: the smell. The combination of scented candles in every room and Helene's gorgeous perfume means that her house smells divine and this is the finishing touch to a cleverly curated home.

OPPOSITE Leading off the kitchen is the dining room featuring a large glossy black circular dining table. The room is filled with candles of all shapes and sizes that Helene lights every night to create a magical dining experience. We love the combination of mismatched chairs and the statement beaded chandelier hanging above the table.

RIGHT The Rockett St George Brass and Smoke table lamp and a star-shaped candleholder catch the light beautifully while the three vintage sieves hanging on the wall are a genius example of elevating everyday objects into artworks by putting them on display. You could replicate this look with shallow baskets or oversized ceramic plates.

LEFT Helene and Robin are lucky enough to have a large hall with wonderful glazed doors and tall skirting boards/base boards. The metal console table is a natural home for a vase of fresh flowers and other carefully chosen pieces. Hanging above it is an oversized mirror – perfectly positioned so you can check your appearance when leaving the house.

ABOVE At first glance this lovely sculpture appears abstract, but it is in fact a carving of a mouth. It sits on a narrow mantelpiece alongside a shallow wooden bowl overflowing with jewellery and a favourite Jérôme Dreyfuss leopard-print clutch bag.

THIS PAGE The sitting room is a study in black and white with subtle touches of gold and green. Helene is skilled at styling tabletops and each one here is a treat for the eyes. The varying textures of the sheepskins, coral and lush ferns add depth and warmth to the room while the use of modern artwork brings a slightly subversive edge. The combination of table lamps, wall lamps and a ceiling light offer a lighting option for every occasion.

THIS PAGE The master bedroom has a wonderfully serene feel with soft linen sheets in natural shades, dark metal stars hung above the bed and a vintage picture of a Madonna and child. Industrial-style lamps sit on painted bedside tables – both functional and beautiful.

BELOW Helene's daughter Claudia has a stylish teenager's bedroom. Rockett St George Benni cushions are piled high on cotton sheets on her vintage iron bed. A pale grey feathered Juju hat hangs above a delicate string of lights and a tiny black and gold dreamcatcher. It's no surprise that Elvis the Jack Russell has decided to have a snooze here.

RIGHT Helene has hung a beautiful chandelier above her bath – an incredibly luxurious feature that transforms the space. Bathroom and shower lighting is subject to special regulations and it is not possible to fit an exposed bulb in a bathroom, but you could opt for a candle chandelier to achieve the same wonderful effect. The sprigs of eucalyptus by the bath provides a gorgeous scent and the Aesop products are a bathtime treat.

BELOW RIGHT Helene and Robin are lucky enough to have a dressing room. As you can imagine, being a boutique owner means that Helene's wardrobe is second to none As with her interiors, when it comes to clothes she likes to mix vintage finds with modern pieces. We particularly coveted this vintage coat.

LEFT Tina's love of typography and signs is a theme that runs throughout her Hove apartment. This little bowl, which has been planted with a pretty succulent, is perfect as Tina loves to call everyone 'darling'.

RIGHT More creative planting ideas. Upon a pile of old Indian chapati boards, a spiny succulent has been planted in a vintage French pepper tin while the spiky cactus has taken up residence in a tarnished metal cup.

CABINET OF *Curiosities*

OPPOSITE Tina's kitchen is faithful to her exuberant personality. She has exposed the brick walls and added floating wooden shelves that hold a collection of vintage signs and tins together along with cooking oils and everyday crockery. Tina hung three mismatching glass chandeliers above the work area and is the lucky owner of a glossy black Smeg fridge. A green vintage medical trolley offers industrial-style open storage.

Every once in a while we meet someone who is so fabulous that we just have to know what their home is like! Never has this desire been as strong as when Tina B first joined the Rockett St George team. With a degree in textiles and a colourful career that includes dressing at Glyndebourne, retail and styling, Tina's natural creativity is evident both at home and in her career. Describing herself as obsessive when it comes to her home, her apartment in Hove, East Sussex is filled with vintage finds that she has meticulously collected over the years. And, just as we expected, Tina's home is every bit as fabulous as Tina herself.

Tina's apartment is in a building that dates back to the mid-18th century and was converted into flats in the 1980s. When done badly, a conversion can destroy a building's architectural integrity. Fortunately, here the Victorian features of the property were retained, allowing Tina to enhance them while adding her very own Tina-esque charm.

The front door opens into a spacious hallway hung with Tina's collection of framed Mona Lisa prints. The original flooring adds interest to this space and the bedroom also enjoys period features, with high ceilings, moulded cornices/crown moldings and a bay window. In here, the wooden floor is covered with cowhides and a huge freestanding

LEFT Tina is a born collector and a skilful curator. She creates striking displays that always have a sense of fun. Here, champagne flutes and Kilner jars sit side by side with tiny dolls, religious statuettes, a pink glitter deer and yet more vintage signs.

OPPOSITE ABOVE LEFT Tina's kitchen is brimming with unusual and beautifully styled utensils next to quirky signs and messages. Our favourite has to be a tea tray bearing the legend 'What A Mess'. Tina has a penchant for religious iconography and has two crucifixes as part of her kitchen display.

OPPOSITE ABOVE RIGHT We love these two vintage-style storage boxes, to which Tina has added the words 'Bits' and 'Bobs'.

OPPOSITE Tina's vintage glass cabinet is a masterclass in how to display collections in a beautiful, practical and fun way. The cupboard itself is very beautiful; made from dark wood, it features a mirrored interior that reflects the light and illuminates the contents. This cabinet is home to Tina's Biba bottle collections, various vintage bottles and vases. A Jonathan Adler candle sits next to stacks of teacups, one of course bearing the letter 'T'.

armoire that Tina painted black adds quirky charm to the room. Above the bed is an ornate mantelshelf that's home to an assortment of vintage artworks and cheeky signs and at the foot of the bed is an exquisite two-seater velvet sofa. A vintage chest of drawers sits in front of the huge bay window.

The living room is bursting with theatrical charm. Stacks of *Vogue* magazines line the shelves (Tina has collected every issue since 1983), embellished here and there with Barbie dolls and fairground ornaments. A purple velvet sofa faces the fireplace, which is adorned with candlesticks, glass domes full of dolls' heads and an oversized metal star. Behind the sofa, a cabinet of curiosities is filled with vintage kitsch and a display of treasured David Bowie magazines. Next door, the kitchen features an exposed brick wall, floating shelves and glass ceiling lights that complete the vintage-emporium effect.

Tina's space is a true reflection of her individuality and creative spirit. By allowing her collections to take centre stage, she has given her home an irrepressible humour and warmth that is truly irresistible.

LEFT Although Tina's house is brimming with her treasures, it never feels cluttered or cramped. Due to the high ceilings and large windows of the Victorian building, the apartment feels peaceful and bright. Tina chose to position her dining table in the bay window overlooking the garden. The Tulip table belonged to her mother and holds many happy memories.

OPPOSITE Adjacent to the bay window is a wall housing a large fireplace and two custom-built shelving units. Tina sprayed the two Benny Bear side tables gold and placed them either side of the fireplace. On the mantelpiece, dolls' heads are piled high beneath glass display domes and a giant wooden star is a focal point. The shelves are home to Tina's magazines and books. A large black cowhide and a vintage glass coffee table filled with illustrated books cover the wooden floor.

OPPOSITE Tina's sense of humour continues into her bedroom, with tongue-in-cheek signs hanging above her bed. Tina is a great lover of cats and has two, Mrs Kensington and Spanky. She chose the Rory Dobner cat cushions for her bed and a mixture of traditional and modern artwork for the walls. We love the cat-eye spectacles eye mask hanging by her bedside table.

LEFT Tina's bedroom boasts a full wall of fitted cupboards that hold her clothes. Selected items, however, are kept out on display, with her handbags hanging from a ladder and creating an eye-catching feature. Monochrome sheepskins cover a vintage bedroom chair.

BELOW In the bay window Tina has placed a beautiful chest that came from an old shop. Covered in handpainted labels, it feeds Tina's love of typography perfectly. A vintage armchair features a cushion bearing the words 'London Kills Me' while the other is home to a handmade doll of Tina herself, created for her by a close friend.

ABOVE Tina's brooch-studded mannequin is a very personal piece that's a constant reminder of days gone by. Tina's favourite is the Vivienne Westwood diamante orb, which sits in pride of place in the centre of the mannequin.

MAKE A STATEMENT

TURN *Heads*

This chapter focuses on ways to create the wow factor. We have put together four tried-and-tested ways to create simply fabulous features that will elevate any interior from great to breathtaking.

1 CREATE IMPACT WITH COLOUR

A great trick for creating drama in a space is to throw in a colourful surprise. And by far the easiest and most cost-effective way to achieve this is with a can of paint. A bright piece of furniture really grabs attention, so be daring and paint a chair hot pink, your fireplace yellow or the kitchen table gold... but beware: painting furniture can be strangely addictive and you may find it hard to stop!

If you have a bigger budget, we would suggest that you invest in a piece of boldly coloured furniture. At the moment, a yellow velvet chair would be at the top of our wish lists. As you know, we both love a brooding, inky colour palette and a vibrant item will really pop against a dark backdrop.

Another great way to introduce a bold flash of colour is in the shape of soft furnishings. The golden floor-to-ceiling curtains in the Paris apartment we photographed for this book (see pages 94-101) were simply remarkable, creating a sunshine effect whatever the weather.

2 GIANT ARTWORK – THE BEST TALKING POINT EVER!

Giant anything creates an impact (we even got excited when the giant crumpet hit the shelves in our local supermarket). Oversized artwork is always a talking point, conveys huge amounts of personality and looks spectacular. Not everyone has huge amounts of cash to spend on art (us included), so we suggest you pay a visit to the nearest craft superstore, buy the largest canvas you can find and go for it... unleash your inner Picasso!

Alternatively, just invest in a stick of glue. Jane recently spent a happy Sunday afternoon with two packs of Christian Lacroix playing cards, a large piece of mount board and some glue, and the result is absolutely stunning. She stuck the playing cards (each one featuring a different Lacroix design) in rows on the board and then teamed the end result with the right off-the-shelf frame. We could look at the end result for hours – it is beautiful and cost very little to put together.

If you do have any spare cash, however, we would suggest that you invest in a piece of art that you really love. Art, like music, is life-enhancing – it creates a mood and you can fall in love with a piece. And the best part of buying art is that it can be sold if you change your mind about it – that's what they call a win-win situation!

OPPOSITE Michael Minns' house is a masterclass in making a statement. Not only is he a magpie when it comes to sourcing amazing pieces, but he also has a knack for colour. Notice how the blue of the chair is echoed in the artwork behind and the white of the vases is repeated in the chair on the right.

ABOVE This brightly coloured fireplace in Niki Jones' Victorian home was an act of creative genius by interior designers The Vawdrey House. We love the pop of yellow and blue against the Cole & Son Flamingo wallpaper. The effect is one of modern sophistication and playfulness: the perfect combination for a family home.

ABOVE RIGHT The gold velvet curtains in Quentin Leroux's home are repeated in different rooms, making them both a bold design statement and a recurrent motif that links the apartment.

RIGHT Shelley Carline created a dining booth within her hallway. She clad the walls in wood to define the space and added pieces of statement art as a final decorative touch.

THIS PAGE Helene Morris' fireplace is an eclectic treasure trove of decorative accessories, photographs and artwork, creating a seriously cool style spot that is testament to Helene's styling skills. The large antique gilt mirror is a bold statement that anchors the arrangement and provides a backdrop to the prized possessions on Helene's mantelpiece.

3 STATEMENT WALLS

You may be surprised to see that we are encouraging statement walls and I don't blame you. We are definitely not fans of one wallpapered wall as a small nod to being unique. Absolutely not. We would always recommend going for it and wallpapering a whole room (wallpaper the ceiling too while you're at it – it can look amazing). But there are occasions when a statement wall can work, and this is mainly due to the amazing *trompe l'oeil* wallpapers on the market at the moment. The designs on offer are incredible – wallpaper designs have never been as exciting. If you would like a wood-clad wall you can have one. If you want giant flowers, a mountain view, ornate cornicing/moldings, antique Chinese paintings, corrugated iron, tin tiles, or whatever else your heart desires, it's all out there. We talk a lot more about this in Chapter 3 (on pages 52–55), but we couldn't do a chapter on making a statement without giving wallpaper a mention.

4 STATEMENT PIECES

A statement piece is an incredible item that surprises, delights and stops you in your tracks – you could describe it as a piece with the wow factor. Think bright red telephone box in the hallway, statue in the kitchen, pinball machine in the sitting room, oversized chandelier in the bathroom or giant mirrored disco ball in the bedroom. These items can range from a beautiful antique mirror or a dramatic statement chair to a downright bonkers faux zebra galloping out of the wall.

ABOVE LEFT True to her theatrical spirit, in her hallway Tina B has opted for a show-stopping display of her collection of reproduction Mona Lisa prints.

ABOVE CENTRE Michael Minns' bathroom is a work of art. The vintage freestanding tub is decadently accompanied by a beautiful glass chandelier suspended from a framework of scaffolding tubes. It's a completely unique idea and the effect is mesmerising – evidence of Michael's remarkable creative talent.

ABOVE RIGHT Michael Minns' house is full of character and excitement from the moment you walk through the door The quirky zebra head hanging by the front door is one of the first sights that greet you and gives a good indication of what is to come!

OPPOSITE Niki's kitchen is a great example of a well-thought out design. Not only is it stylish and beautiful, it's also a practical, family- friendly space. We particularly love the Midas Bar Stools (a bit of shameless Rockett St George self-promotion!) which seamlessly combine with the deep navy walls and cabinets.

PLAYFUL YET
Sophisticated

If you are tempted by sweeping grounds, stately rooms, traditional features and modern twists, then this is the house for you. Crunching up the gravel drive to the large, white-painted Victorian house, its fabulous hot-pink front door immediately captures the eye. Located in Kent's Tunbridge Wells, the magnificent building had been divided into two dwellings in the 1950s, and when Niki Jones and her husband Kenton bought the house they faced the significant challenge of knocking them both back into a house. Niki decided to enlist the help of interior designers The Vawdrey House and together they worked hard to restore this imposing house to its original grandeur.

Downstairs, the refurbished and extended house has two regal reception rooms, a large kitchen and dining space that opens onto the garden, and a study, a utility room and a garage. Upstairs are five bedrooms and three bathrooms, all accessed from a light-filled stairwell, while the cellar is home to a playroom, wine store, spare bedroom and plant room.

ABOVE Niki's hallway is spacious and bright, creating a calm and welcoming feeling. The dark paintwork on the glass double doors and the skirting boards/base boards gives the architectural features definition and draws attention to the height of the ceiling.

OPPOSITE There is so much to love about the kitchen/dining area in Niki's house. The use of colour is inspired, with the bright blue door and the odd yellow chair dotted around the table. The effect is striking and conjures up a relaxed, family-friendly atmosphere. The cluster of assorted pendant lights hanging above the dining table strikes a glamorous note and the different shapes and lengths really grab the eye.

LEFT The study, just off the kitchen, is a tranquil chillout zone. The pop of yellow against the white walls and floor brings a flash of colour.

BELOW Niki's sitting room is full of fabulous style spots. A decorative side table is home to a carefully curated collection of glass vases of different sizes and shapes while the glazed cabinet behind the sofa contains vintage glassware and has an artwork and vase of flowers perched on top.

The front door opens into a high-ceilinged hallway that leads to a dark reception room with brightly coloured furniture, a log-burning stove and a mirrored drinks cabinet that can be concealed behind a door. The charcoal walls create a sense of drama and intimacy, making this the perfect space for entertaining.

From here a door leads into a bright modern kitchen with large glass sliding doors overlooking the garden. The stunning blue-black cabinets are the perfect backdrop for Niki's collection of ceramics, and her copper sink is to die for. A pocket door painted turquoise closes off a study area with a pitched roof and window seat.

From the hall, a staircase leads up to the bedrooms. The master suite features floor-to-ceiling fitted wardrobes (the dream, in our

LEFT There is nothing that delights us more than the uncompromising embrace of the dark side! Niki has opted for deep navy walls in her reception room and the sober shade only serves to highlight the alluring sparkle of the mirrored bar area.

RIGHT The gorgeous pink velvet banquette seating and hot pink candles are complemented by flashes of gold in Niki's reception room, creating an effect of effortless sophistication. We like the minimalist look of this room, as it allows feature pieces such as the cocktail chair and the pineapple wall sconces to really stand out.

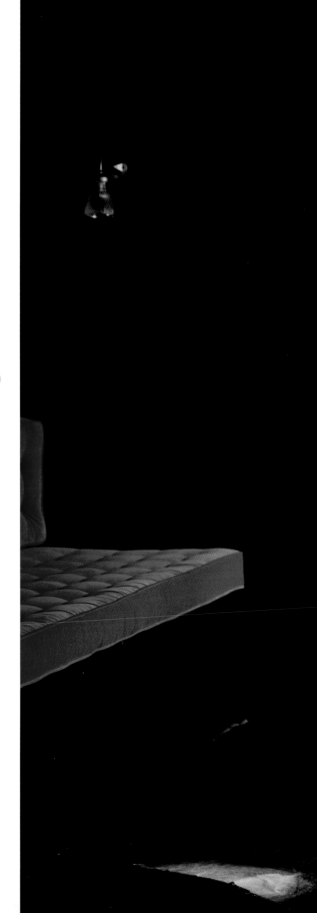

opinion), dark blue walls and soft pink and blue accessories. Niki has used sheepskins, candles and flowers to add interest and texture and create a relaxing atmosphere. We love the vintage glass lights either side of the bed. The sleek en-suite bathrooms are fully tiled in neutral hues with lighting and accessories adding vibrant pops of colour.

The top floor houses the children's bedrooms and a spare room, together with another bathroom. The children's rooms burst with fun and personality and Niki chose a combination of wallpaper, paint and murals to add the wow factor to each space.

This house is the perfect combination of sophisticated style and family comfort. It is has spectacular architectural features yet the unexpected modern twists throughout add charm and humour, resulting in an absolutely beautiful home.

LEFT In the sitting room, interior designers The Vawdrey House kept the décor simple to accentuate the beauty of the large Victorian bay windows, which are complete with their original shutters. The sheepskin on the rocking chair creates a cosy vibe while the geometric side table adds a modern twist. The whole room is tied together by low-level lighting, which creates a magical effect at night.

BELOW The colour scheme in the master bedroom creates a cool, laid-back vibe that's both playful and sophisticated. We love the ceiling lights that hang either side of the bed – they are a great alternative to a traditional bedside lamp. The Rockett St George glass cage lantern creates a cosy feeling and looks wonderful at night when the candle is lit.

RIGHT AND BELOW RIGHT A vintage armchair dressed with a cosy sheepskin and pink cushion is a chic twist on the traditional and we particularly love the vintage floor light hanging nearby, which makes this corner into a brilliant style spot. The feather dressing hanging over the mirror is another favourite of ours and adds an exotic twist to the room's sleek modern decor.

WORK IN PROGRESS 8

ALWAYS *Evolving*

You may have noticed that throughout this book, we keep revisiting the theory that homes and their interior design should be an extension of the owner's personality. Please excuse the repetition, but we genuinely believe that if you are to create a home that you love, your interior decoration must be firmly rooted in your individual personality and style.

LEFT Rather than using the space adjacent to her kitchen to house a dining table, Shelley Carline chose to turn it into a cosy snug centred on a log burner. This was without a doubt the right decision, as it is the perfect spot to sit, enjoy a glass of wine and be where the action is.

OPPOSITE Cowboy Kate decided to use individual pieces of furniture rather than opting for a fitted kitchen and the result is spectacular. Glossy black metro tiles sit above a butler's sink, large storage baskets sit snugly beneath the various work surfaces and pots and pans are piled high on a butcher's block. The plants and wall lights are the perfect finishing touches.

With this in mind, it is important to remember that, as time goes by, things change. We grow as people, our tastes develop in different ways, families mature and their makeup changes. Our interiors should change too, reflecting the new but also retaining the best from the past. So often, we move to a new home and see the interior design process as a finite one. It is very easy to view your home as a project to be undertaken as quickly as possible and to believe that when it's finished it will be finished forever. But this will never be the case. Every home is a work in progress and the interiors should grow and develop along with the occupants. We like to think of a home as a place that needs to be continually improved and tweaked, with things constantly being removed and added to suit your current lifestyle.

If, like us, you love interior design, this should be great news for you. We don't need any excuses to be constantly adding to our homes. It is a wonderful opportunity to enjoy the incredibly pleasing creative process of making your space special and personal.

LEFT In Cowboy Kate's dining room, a dramatic artwork of a horse echoes the rich mahogany hue of the rare-breed sheepskins that cover the dining chairs, adding warmth and depth to the room. The wall features a distressed gold paint effect that is a decorating triumph and beautifully echoes the sparkling glass chandelier.

OPPOSITE ABOVE Cowboy Kate has an amazing eye and each part of her sitting room is a carefully considered style spot. The monochrome portraits by Gill Button above the black leather sofa create an eye-catching effect and the lampshades and sheepskins are in similar tones to the artwork so the whole space blends together perfectly.

OPPOSITE BELOW Tina B used a salvaged piece of architectural cornicing/crown molding to create a display shelf above her bed. She has chosen quirky art and some rather naughty rulers to fill the space.

One thing we would emphasize here is to hang onto those special items that make up the story of your life. Don't be tempted to completely clear out and start again. Jane made this mistake and mourns the loss of her mother's Ercol table that she owned in her first flat. On the plus side, she was wise enough to hold on to a blanket box that originally belonged to her grandmother who had it made especially to act as her 'bottom drawer' before she married. Display keepsakes from your changing lives and arrange them in ways that make you smile, however big or small they might be. These are important pieces that can never be replaced and should be kept – they are not only beautiful objects but they also remind us of good times and important people in our lives.

So there you have it: our first book. We have thoroughly enjoyed the process of creating it and feel honoured to have been given the opportunity to visit and photograph so many incredible homes and meet such creative people. Hopefully we have imparted some helpful tips and ideas that will inspire you to continue to create your own extraordinary interiors!

LEFT Lucy and Paul's kitchen was designed for maximum sociability. She wanted to have the hob/stovetop on the island to allow her to face family and guests while she cooks. Perfect for a fun-loving hostess.
RIGHT Flooded with natural light from large windows and a skylight, the kitchen is bright and welcoming. The polished concrete floor and modern kitchen fittings are simple and stylish. Lucy and Paul used wall-hung display shelves to inject a sense of personality and fun into the space.

ECLECTIC *Glamour*

Staying true to the sentiment that Rockett St George was built on – 'we only buy what we love' – Lucy St George's home is filled with exquisite vintage pieces that tell of her individuality. A treasure-hunter by nature, in her home Lucy has managed to achieve what so many people struggle with: she has allowed the architecture speak for itself but without diluting her unique sense of style.

Lucy and her family – husband Paul and their children Ella, Grace and Ollie – live in a three-storey semi-detached house in North London. With its high ceilings, broad hallways and landings and original wooden floors, the house is a classic example of traditional Edwardian architecture. Step through the front door and you are greeted by a large hallway, a double living room and an open-plan kitchen/dining room that leads onto the garden. Upstairs are their children's bedrooms and bathrooms while on the very top floor is the master bedroom, bathroom and dressing room.

True to her glamour goddess spirit, Lucy's house is an eclectic mix of one-off finds from eBay, flea markets and car-boot sales combined with Rockett St George pieces

RIGHT AND BELOW
Lucy's vintage Saarinen Tulip dining table looks fabulous surrounded by Eames DSW chairs and a vintage leather bus seat. They do say that all the fun happens on the back seat! She added drama to the space by hanging a huge vintage railway mirror between large palms.

A small act is worth
a million thoughts.

both old and new. There's no better place to find a rock 'n' roll vibe than Lucy's living room. The walls are painted deepest navy blue, sheepskins are scattered over the sofas, fairground lights are dotted on the floor, plants are dressed with strings of tree lights and quirky animal ornaments, oversized artwork and mirrors cover the walls.

Packed with such treasures, including Paul's vintage drinks cabinet, Lucy and Paul's home could look cluttered but they successfully navigate this risk. How, you may ask? Well, it's partly down to a little Lucy magic and partly due to her clever use of style spots. Style spots are a key feature of almost every room in Lucy's home and they really express her personality. Playing with different heights and textures

OPPOSITE In the sitting room, inky blue walls work perfectly with metallic accessories and pale leather sofas. The cherub statue was a gift and holds court amongst piles of cushions and plants.

ABOVE The dark walls are the perfect backdrop for the rich, mellow tones of dark wood furniture and leafy palms. A black convex mirror hangs above the fireplace.

RIGHT On the upstairs landing, Lucy applied a stained glass-effect window film to a pair of glass doors to add colour and pattern to the otherwise monochrome scheme. Window film is inexpensive and easy to use and the results are striking. This design is Flutterby by Christin Yu for Purlfrost.

means that you never know quite what might be around the next corner. It also means that the house's original features are enhanced: the elegant original Victorian fireplaces are focal points while quirky accent lighting illuminates the art on the walls and ceilings and windows have been opened up to let the natural light pour in.

Most importantly, the imaginative and playful decor oozes fun and warmth and makes Lucy and Paul's home a unique place for their family to grow up in. Add to that a dash of glam and glitter and a sprinkle of naughty humour and Lucy has created the perfect home for herself and her family.

LEFT Floating shelves of varying lengths offer a great display opportunity in Ella St George's bedroom. She has covered them with a collection of framed pictures and photographs plus a Rockett St George LED pink neon heart. The cushions scattered on the floor and a quirky 'Happynest' lightbox combine to make this the perfect teenage hangout.

ABOVE AND OPPOSITE Lucy and Paul's bedroom is a study in greys and blues. The view from the window is spectacular and this armchair is the perfect spot from which to enjoy the views of Alexandra Palace. Rockett St George pineapple table lamps adorn the black and gold bedside tables and the bed is dressed in soft blue linen bedding and black linen cushions.

MINIMALIST *Magic*

Describing his style as 'laid-back minimalism', Fred Musik epitomizes creative cool. During the course of an exciting and varied career, he worked as a freelancer and a magazine designer and ran his own restaurant with his partner Mark. Recently, Fred, Mark and their three French bulldogs have moved into a Victorian townhouse in Hove that had not been touched since the 1960s. The house is a huge five-floor, seven-bedroom project but we can think of no one more suited to such a momentous enterprise than Fred and Mark.

Appreciative of the Victorian property's natural features, Fred has carefully retained the period townhouse's original features and combined this with minimalist decor and quirky furnishings to create an effortless, laid-back vibe. Once through the front door, your eyes are instantly drawn to the hall's elaborate plaster cornices/crown moldings, marbled pillars and spectacular gilded ceiling light. Moving into the living room, the clean white walls create a feeling of calm

ABOVE LEFT This small style spot occupies Fred and Mark's kitchen worksurface. It is composed of a plant, glass storage jar, a beautiful blue Chinese Foo dog and an ethnic-inspired piece of art. Together the items create visual interest and add personality to the space.

ABOVE CENTRE Fred and Mark's home is filled with beautiful traditional features such as these stunning tiles, which we found on an upstairs fireplace. It is the combination of traditional features and modern accessories that make this house so breathtaking.

ABOVE RIGHT The original Victorian plaster cornicing/crown molding in the hallway is stunning. Fred and Mark have hung a beautiful vintage ceiling light here and added a marble paint effect to the pillars.

OPPOSITE The brave choice of lilac for the kitchen cabinets is inspiring. We love the combination of the lilac with the gold sofa and vivid green velvet cushion. The colours all sit comfortably alongside each other, as do Mark and Fred's three French bulldogs as they relax and wait for dinner to be served.

simplicity and allow the attention-grabbing statement furniture to do all the talking. Plush teal velvet sofas sit on deep pile rugs, a mirrored glass ball light sits on the floor and an ornate gilt mirror is propped up on the marble fireplace.

The kitchen is proof that Fred is not afraid to take risks. The sleek modern cabinets have an unexpected twist – they are a striking lilac shade. In both colour and form they offer a complete contrast to the upholstered gold sofa and antique wooden armoire positioned by the back door. To accommodate such a striking difference, Fred has carefully kept the rest of the decor simple.

Moving on to the master bed and bathroom, we were transfixed by the glorious floor-to-ceiling windows and perfectly preserved Victorian ceiling mouldings. The furniture here is a genius combination of modern retro armchairs, a carved wooden chimneypiece and a Chinese-style painted screen, while the fiddle-leaf fig adds a vibrant splash of green. As with the bedroom, the master bathroom is a skilful

OPPOSITE ABOVE
The sitting room includes a combination of modern classics, such as the Ligne Roset Togo sofa in forest green, and traditional pieces, such as the gold-framed mirror above the fireplace. Record decks are placed casually on a pile of magazines and a mirrored coffee table houses a collection of books. The oversized paper lantern emphasises the stunning scale and grandeur of the room.

OPPOSITE BELOW
Album covers are quite often works of art and this Diana Ross album is no exception.

RIGHT Fred and Mark's home has incredible skirting boards/base boards, which are to be coveted (Jane has always wanted tall skirting boards; it is a strange thing to desire). We love the simplicity of this corner featuring a pretty two-armed vintage wall light, a simple retro-style chair and a John Lennon artwork.

The dark grey paint that covers the walls, woodwork and ceiling of this bedroom creates a rich and cocooning feel. The effect is wonderfully calming, so much so that this would definitely be our choice of bedroom if we were fortunate enough to own this beautiful house.

ABOVE LEFT AND RIGHT The master bathroom is divided into two parts; the first housing a 1920s bath that Fred and Mark discovered in a field and had re-enamelled. Opposite is a fireplace alongside a large vintage industrial cabinet filled with towels and luxe toiletries. The second part of the room houses a double shower opposite a double sink unit. It really is the perfect bathroom.

RIGHT The bedroom on the top floor has been painted a glorious charcoal grey. The space is simple and peaceful, featuring a double bed, chaise longue and decorative table.

combination of old and new. The ceiling was stripped back to the original plaster and Fred and Mark found an old 1920s bath and had it re-enamelled. A large glazed display cabinet, molecular ceiling light and vintage clock provide the finishing touches.

As you climb up to the top floor, the mood changes from light, bright and minimal to rich, dark and sumptuous. The bedroom here features rich charcoal walls, subtle gold accents, candlelight, dark bedding and a decorative metal and glass wheatsheaf table. A pink velvet armchair completes the look.

Staying faithful to his own personal style, Fred has created a home that is a testament to his creative vision. Such a remarkable house really should be shared and luckily Fred and Mark think so too – they have decided to let the property out on Airbnb and we think it's well worth a visit!

THIS PAGE The master bedroom on the first floor features a floor-to-ceiling bay window, and what better to fill it than a vintage Karuselli lounge chair teamed with a Chinese screen, a spaceman print and an oversized mirror ball. The combination of items is unique and they work perfectly together, representing the eclectic style and personality of the owners.

ABOVE The magnificent original fireplace in the main bedroom has been carefully restored and makes a spectacular feature. Fred and Mark chose a low divan bed that does not detract from the fireplace and accentuates the size and height of the room.

ABOVE RIGHT Statement artwork is always a great interior design move and a brilliant way to bring personality to an interior. This vintage Grace Jones poster hits you right between the eyes... in a good way!

RIGHT On the upstairs landing, a small alcove lit by a stained-glass window is the perfect place for a style spot composed of a simple vintage plywood chair, a black Anglepoise lamp and a tall glass display dome housing a split rock of crystal.

SOURCES

LONDON

2&4
2–4 Southgate Road
London N1 3JW
+44 (0)20 7254 5202
2mdesign.co.uk
*Modern furniture and
art together with tea
and cakes.*

Abigail Ahern
12–14 Essex Road
London N1 8LN
+44 (0)20 7354 8181
abigailahern.com
*A veritable treasure trove
of wonders for the home.*

Bow Arts Open Studios
183 Bow Road
London E3 2SJ
+44 (0)20 8980 7774
bowarts.org
*The first choice for
emerging artists and
London's leading arts and
creative learning provider.*

Chiswick Car Boot Sale
Chiswick School
Burlington Lane
London W4 3UN
chiswickcarbootsale.com
*Open on the first Sunday
of every month, this car
boot sale is a great place
to treasure hunt.*

The Conran Shop
Michelin House
81 Fulham Road
London SW3 6RD
+44 (0)20 7589 7401
conranshop.co.uk
*Worth visiting for the
building alone, this shop
is the daddy of interior
stores offering the very
best of modern design.*

Cockpit Arts
Open Studios
Cockpit Yard
Northington St
London WC1N 2NP
+44 (0)20 7419 1959
and at
18–22 Creekside
London SE8 3DZ
cockpitarts.com
*Visit one of these two
studios to see behind the
scenes in the studios and
to buy work direct from
the resident craftspeople
and artist-makers.*

Columbia Road
Flower Market
Columbia Road
London E2 7RG
columbiaroad.info
*The perfect way to spend
a Sunday.*

Craft Central
21 Clerkenwell Green
London EC14 0DX
and at
33–35 St John's Square
London EC1M 4DS
craftcentral.org.uk
*Hosts the Made In
Clerkenwell exhibition –
a biannual celebration of
the work of Craft Central
resident designer makers.*

Harvey Nichols
109–125 Knightsbridge
London SW1X 7RJ
+44 (0)207 235 5000
harveynichols.com
*Simply fabulous, sweetie
darling!*

Heals
The Heal's Building
196 Tottenham Court Road
London W1T 7LQ
+44 (0)20 7419 1959
heals.com
*Specializes in great design
and well-made products.*

Liberty
Regent Street
London W1B 5AH
+44 (0)20 7734 1234
libertylondon.com
*This historic and beautifully
curated department store
offers everything from
fashion to furnishing
fabrics and crafts.*

The Old Cinema
160 Chiswick High Road
London W4 1PR
+44 (0)20 8995 4166
theoldcinema.co.uk
*Fantastic antique,
vintage and retro
furniture specialist.*

Pure White Lines
45 Hackney Road
London E2 7NX
+44 (0)20 3222 0137
purewhitelines.com
*One-stop shop for
spectacular pieces with
a fast-changing stock, so
there is always something
exciting and new.*

SUSSEX

Ardingly Antiques Fair
South of England
   Showground
Ardingly
Nr Haywards Heath
West Sussex RH17 6TL
iacf.co.uk/ardingly
*The perfect place to
watch the sun rise and
find unique pieces for your
home. Get there early!*

Butler's Emporium
70 George Street
Hastings TN34 3EE
+44 (0)1424 430678
*Located in the heart of
Hastings Old Town, this
shop dates from about
1832 and offers a curated
collection of homeware
and gifts.*

McCully & Crane
27b Cinque Ports Street
Rye
East Sussex TN31 7AD
+44 (0)7932 478383
mccullyandcrane.com
You know that perfect piece of art you are always looking out for? You will find it here.

No.1 Lewes
1 Cliffe High Street
Lewes
East Sussex BN7 2AH
+44 (0)1273 477714
theshoplewes.co.uk
Wonderful antiques. On the pricey side, but you will not regret a purchase made here.

Swag 91
91 Trafalgar Street
Brighton BN1 4ER
+44 (0)1273 688504
swagantiques.com
A wide range of antiques, retro, vintage and decorative pieces in a contemporary setting.

PARIS

Merci
111 Boulevard Beaumarchais
75003 Paris
France
+33 1 42 77 00 33
merci-merci.com
The concept store of all concept stores. Always full of wonderful thing to buy and eat.

La Maison Pernoise Concept Store
167 Avenue de la Gare
84210 Pernes-les-Fontaines
France
+33 9 81 45 04 22
lamaisonpernoise.com
A great place to find Moroccan homeware and other treats.

NEW YORK

ABC Carpet and Home
888 Broadway
New York NY 10003
abchome.com
Visit this shop for the breathtaking displays and gorgeous products. It's a must when in New York.

Brooklyn Flea Market
On Saturdays in
Williamsburg
90 Kent Ave
Brooklyn, NY 11211
And on Sunday at Brooklyn
Manhattan Bridge Archway
80 Pearl Street
brooklynflea.com
An unmissable experience.

BERLIN

Arkonaplatz Flea Market
Arkonaplatz
10435 Berlin Prenzlauer
Berg
Germany
troedelmarkt-arkonaplatz.de
A lively outdoor market filled with vintage clothing, antiques and wonderful art.

Hotel Ultra Concept Store
Torstrasse 155
10115 Berlin
+49 30 27 58 11 00
hotelultra.de
A quirky and fun-filled design store.

REYKJAVIK

Magnolia
Skólavörðustíg 38
101 Reykjavík
A wonderful collection of homeware and art.

MARRAKESH

Bazar Kassri
3 Souk Dylaouine
(Près des Teinturies)
Marrakech
4000
Morocco
bazarkassri.com
The best place to buy blankets.

Poterie de Tamegroute
28 Rue Mouassine
Medina
Marrakech
4000
Morocco
A great place to buy the wonderful green ceramics crafted in Tamegroute in Morocco's deep south.

Soufiane Zarib
20db Amsgi Rehbael
Kadima
Marrakech
40040
Morocco
The best place to buy rugs.

AUSTRALIA

The Society Inc
302/75 Mary Street
St Peters 2044
Australia
+61 (0)2 9516 5643
thesocietyinc.com.au
Run by interior designer Sibella Court, this shop offers a beautifully curated collection of modern accessories mixed with vintage finds.

Ahoy Trader
Shop 1/3 Marvell Street
Byron Bay
NSW 2481
Australia
+61 (0)2 6680 7764
ahoytrader.com
Beautiful homeware store featuring stunning artwork by Jai Vasicek.

PICTURE CREDITS

KEY r = right, l = left, c = centre, br = below right, bl = below left, al = above left, ar = above right.

1 The family home of Quentin Leroux in Paris, designed by Royal Roulotte www.royalroulotte.com; 2 The home of Katherine Jane Learmonth of www.cowboykate.co.uk in North Yorkshire; 3 The family home of Jane Rockett and Toby Erlam of Rockett St George; 4 The home of Helene and Robin of Neilson Boutique in Cuckfield, Sussex www.neilsonboutique.co.uk; 5al The family home of Niki and Kenton Jones in Kent, designed by The Vawdrey House www.thevawdreyhouse.com; 5bl The home of Katherine Jane Learmonth of www.cowboykate.co.uk in North Yorkshire; 5r The family home of Lucy St George and Paul Batts of Rockett St George; 7 The home of interior stylist Deborah Vos www.deborahvos.com; 8–9 The home of Katherine Jane Learmonth of www.cowboykate.co.uk in North Yorkshire; 10–11 The family home of Jane Rockett and Toby Erlam of Rockett St George; 12–13 The home of Katherine Jane Learmonth of www.cowboykate.co.uk in North Yorkshire; 14 The family home of Jane Rockett and Toby Erlam of Rockett St George; 16 Tina B; 17bl Michael Minns, East Yorkshire; 17ar The family home of designers Alexandra and Nicolas Valla of Royal Roulotte www.royalroulotte.com; 17br The family home of Niki and Kenton Jones in Kent, designed by The Vawdrey House www.thevawdreyhouse.com; 18–25 The family home of Jane Rockett and Toby Erlam of Rockett St George; 26–33 The family home of designers Alexandra and Nicolas Valla of Royal Roulotte www.royalroulotte.com; 34–35 The home of Shelley Carline, owner of the shop Hilary and Flo in Sheffield; 36 Artist Residence, Brighton; 37 Brody House, Budapest; 39 Mama Shelter, Paris; 40–47 The home of Shelley Carline, owner of the shop Hilary and Flo in Sheffield; 48–49 Michael Minns, East Yorkshire; 50–51a The family home of Jane Rockett and Toby Erlam of Rockett St George; 51b The home of Shelley Carline, owner of the shop Hilary and Flo in Sheffield; 52a The family home of Jane Rockett and Toby Erlam of Rockett St George; 52b The home of Katherine Jane Learmonth of www.cowboykate.co.uk in North Yorkshire; 53al Michael Minns, East Yorkshire; 53ar The family home of Niki and Kenton Jones in Kent, designed by The Vawdrey House www.thevawdreyhouse.com; 53b The family home of Quentin Leroux in Paris, designed by Royal Roulotte www.royalroulotte.com; 55al Michael Minns, East Yorkshire; 55ar and b The family home of Lucy St George and Paul Batts of Rockett St George; 56–65 Michael Minns, East Yorkshire; 66–67 The home of Katherine Jane Learmonth of www.cowboykate.co.uk in North Yorkshire; 68 The family home of Lucy St George and Paul Batts of Rockett St George; 69 The home of Helene and Robin of Neilson Boutique in Cuckfield, Sussex www.neilsonboutique.co.uk; 70l Fred Musik; 70c and r The home of Katherine Jane Learmonth of www.cowboykate.co.uk in North Yorkshire; 71al Fred Musik; 71bl The family home of Lucy St George and Paul Batts of Rockett St George; 71r The family home of Niki and Kenton Jones in Kent, designed by The Vawdrey House www.thevawdreyhouse.com; 72a The home of Helene and Robin of Neilson Boutique in Cuckfield, Sussex www.neilsonboutique.co.uk; 72b The family home of designers Alexandra and Nicolas Valla of Royal Roulotte www.royalroulotte.com; 73 The home of Helene and Robin of Neilson Boutique in Cuckfield, Sussex www.neilsonboutique.co.uk; 74l The family home of Lucy St George and Paul Batts of Rockett St George; 74r The home of Katherine Jane Learmonth of www.cowboykate.co.uk in North Yorkshire; 75–85 The home of Katherine Jane Learmonth of www.cowboykate.co.uk in North Yorkshire; 86 The family home of Quentin Leroux in Paris, designed by Royal Roulotte www.royalroulotte.com; 87 The family home of Niki and Kenton Jones in Kent, designed by The Vawdrey House www.thevawdreyhouse.com; 88 The family home of Lucy St George and Paul Batts of Rockett St George; 89 The family home of Quentin Leroux in Paris, designed by Royal Roulotte www.royalroulotte.com; 90a Michael Minns, East Yorkshire; 90bl The family home of Quentin Leroux in Paris, designed by Royal Roulotte www.royalroulotte.com; 90br The family home of designers Alexandra and Nicolas Valla of Royal Roulotte www.royalroulotte.com; 91 The home of Helene and Robin of Neilson Boutique in Cuckfield, Sussex www.neilsonboutique.co.uk; 92 The family home of Lucy St George and Paul Batts of Rockett St George; 93l Michael Minns, East Yorkshire; 93c The family home of Jane Rockett and Toby Erlam of Rockett St George; 93r The home of Katherine Jane Learmonth of www.cowboykate.co.uk in North Yorkshire; 94–101 The family home of Quentin Leroux in Paris, designed by Royal Roulotte www.royalroulotte.com; 102–109 The home of interior stylist Deborah Vos www.deborahvos.com; 110 The home of Helene and Robin of Neilson Boutique in Cuckfield, Sussex www.neilsonboutique.co.uk; 111 Michael Minns, East Yorkshire; 112 The family home of Jane Rockett and Toby Erlam of Rockett St George; 113l The family home of Lucy St George and Paul Batts of Rockett St George; 113r The family home of designers Alexandra and Nicolas Valla of Royal Roulotte www.royalroulotte.com; 114l and c Tina B; 114r The home of Katherine Jane Learmonth of www.cowboykate.co.uk in North Yorkshire; 115 The family home of Lucy St George and Paul Batts of Rockett St George; 116 Tina B; 117l The family home of Jane Rockett and Toby Erlam of Rockett St George; 117r The home of Shelley Carline, owner of the shop Hilary and Flo in Sheffield; 118–125 The home of Helene and Robin of Neilson Boutique in Cuckfield, Sussex www.neilsonboutique.co.uk; 126–131 Tina B; 134 The family home of Niki and Kenton Jones in Kent, designed by The Vawdrey House www.thevawdreyhouse.com; 135 The home of Katherine Jane Learmonth of www.cowboykate.co.uk in North Yorkshire; 136 Michael Minns, East Yorkshire; 137al The family home of Niki and Kenton Jones in Kent, designed by The Vawdrey House www.thevawdreyhouse.com; 137ar The family home of Quentin Leroux in Paris, designed by Royal Roulotte www.royalroulotte.com; 137b The home of Shelley Carline, owner of the shop Hilary and Flo in Sheffield; 138 The home of Helene and Robin of Neilson Boutique in Cuckfield, Sussex www.neilsonboutique.co.uk; 139al Tina B; 139ac and r Michael Minns, East Yorkshire; 140–147 The family home of Niki and Kenton Jones in Kent, designed by The Vawdrey House www.thevawdreyhouse.com; 148–149 The family home of Lucy St George and Paul Batts of Rockett St George; 150 The home of Shelley Carline, owner of the shop Hilary and Flo in Sheffield; 151–153a The home of Katherine Jane Learmonth of www.cowboykate.co.uk in North Yorkshire; 153b Tina B; 154–161 The family home of Lucy St George and Paul Batts of Rockett St George; 162–169 Fred Musik; 170 Tina B; 171 The family home of designers Alexandra and Nicolas Valla of Royal Roulotte www.royalroulotte.com; 173 The home of interior stylist Deborah Vos www.deborahvos.com; 176l The family home of Quentin Leroux in Paris, designed by Royal Roulotte www.royalroulotte.com; 176c The family home of Jane Rockett and Toby Erlam of Rockett St George; 176r The family home of Niki and Kenton Jones in Kent, designed by The Vawdrey House www.thevawdreyhouse.com.

BUSINESS CREDITS

KEY r = right, l = left, c = centre, br = below right, bl = below left, al = above left, ar = above right.

Artist Residence 36

Brody House, Budapest 37

www.cowboykate.co.uk 2, 5 bl, 8–9, 12–13, 52 b, 66–67, 70c, 70r, 74r, 75–85, 93r, 114r, 135, 151–153.

www.deborahvos.com 7, 102–109, 173.

Hilary and Flo
959 Eccleshall Road
Sheffield S11 8TN
T: 0114 267 0797
www.hilaryandflo.co.uk
34–35, 40–47, 51b, 117r, 137b, 150.

Mama Shelter 39

Neilson Boutique
The Clock House
Cuckfield
Sussex RH17 5JX
T: 01444 416 288
www.neilsonboutique.co.uk
4, 69, 72a, 73, 91, 110, 118–125, 138.

Rockett St George
www.rockettstgeorge.co.uk
3, 5r, 10–11, 14, 18–25, 50, 51a, 52a, 55ar, 55b, 68, 71bl, 74l, 88, 92, 93c, 112, 113l, 115, 117l, 148–149, 154–161, 176c.

Royal Roulotte
www.royalroulotte.com
1, 17ar, 26–33, 53b, 72b, 86, 89, 90bl, 90br, 94–101, 113r, 137ar, 171, 176l.

Shootfactory
T: +44 (0)20 7252 3900
www.shootfactory.co.uk
17bl, 48–49, 53al, 55al, 56–65, 90a, 93l, 111, 136, 139ac, 139r.

The Vawdrey House Ltd
Architecture, Interior Design, Project Management
www.thevawdreyhouse.com
5al, 17br, 53ar, 71r, 87, 134, 137al, 140–147, 176r.

INDEX

Page numbers in *italic* refer to the captions

ACKNOWLEDGMENTS

THANK YOU TO...

The Rockett St George team – Abbie, Cathy, Chloe, David, Ella, Ellie, Elliot, Freya, George, Karen, Katie, Kellie, Laura, Lee, Louise, Luc, Matt, Matt, Mike, Sam, Sophie, Suzanne, Tina, Tom, Tyler, Victoria and Yvonne. Thank you for all your hard work. You are the dream team.

The kids – Ella, Tyler, Lola, Grace, Eden and Ollie. Thank you for your love and 'go get 'em' attitude towards our seventh child, Rockett St George. Thank you for putting up with the constant redecoration and rearrangement of furniture in our homes and for not complaining (too much) when we drag you to car boot sales, interiors shops and markets. We appreciate your unwavering support throughout and we love you very much.

The boys – Toby and Paul. Thank you for all your love, continuous help with keeping the plates spinning, and always having a glass of wine on hand.

The parents – Anne and Chris, Jeffrey and Paula. Thank you for all the dinners, washing and taxi rides for us and now for all the kids. You have always been a great support.

The photographer – Debi Treloar. Thank you for being such a pleasure to work with and understanding so clearly what we wanted to create.

The publishing team – Annabel, Cindy, Jess, Leslie and Toni. Thank you so much for asking us to create this book and guiding us throughout the process. We couldn't have done it without you.

All the home owners – Helene and Robin, Fred and Mark, Tina B, Niki and Kenton, The Vawdrey House, Cowboy Kate/Jane and John, Deborah and Tim, Michael, Shelley, Quentin, and Alexandra and Nicolas. Thank you for letting us into your inspirational and extraordinary homes.

VEGETARIAN

VEGETARIAN

Louise Pickford

hamlyn

First published in Great Britain in 1996
by Hamlyn, a division of Octopus Publishing Group Ltd
2–4 Heron Quays, London E14 4JP

This edition published 2004 by Octopus Publishing Group Ltd

Copyright ©1996, 2004 Octopus Publishing Group Ltd

ISBN 0 600 61112 4

Printed in China

NOTES

Both metric and imperial measurements have been given
in all recipes. Use one set of measurements only and not a
mixture of both.

Standard level spoon measurements are used in all recipes.
1 tablespoon = one 15 ml spoon
1 teaspoon = one 5 ml spoon

Eggs should be medium to large unless otherwise stated.

Milk should be full fat unless otherwise stated.

Pepper should be freshly ground black pepper unless
otherwise stated.

Fresh herbs should be used unless otherwise stated.
If unavailable use dried herbs as an alternative but halve the
quantities stated.

Measurements for canned and tinned food have been given as a
standard metric equivalent.

Ovens should be preheated to the specified temperature
– if using a fan-assisted oven, follow the manufacturer's
instructions for adjusting the time and the temperature.

Contents

Introduction

The vibrant colours and infinitely varied textures and flavours of vegetables, fruits and grains proclaim the benefits of vegetarian cooking. Vegetarianism is not a modern fad: in many countries it is the natural way to eat, and has been so for thousands of years.

Taking its inspiration from around the world, this book uses fresh vegetables, beans, lentils, pasta, rice and many other grains, fruit, eggs and cheese to make delicious meat-free meals that will appeal to the committed vegetarian as well as those who like to eat less meat.

PROTEIN
Protein is needed for the growth and maintenance of all body cells. It is made up of amino acids, some of which are manufactured in our bodies, while others – the essential amino acids – can only be obtained from food. Eggs, milk, yogurt, cheese and soya bean products (such as tofu) contain all these essential amino acids. Beans, peas, lentils, grains, nuts and seeds are valuable sources of protein, but do not contain all the essential amino acids. However, by eating certain foods together, we can obtain all the protein we need. Many combinations are natural partners: hearty soups made with beans and pasta,

lentil curry with rice in India, beans with flour tortillas in Mexico.

CARBOHYDRATES
Carbohydrates provide the body with energy, and divide into two categories: simple and complex. Simple carbohydrates or sugars contribute sweetness but very little else and are sometimes referred to as empty calories; these are to be avoided. Fruit contains plenty of natural sugars, but also contains fibre and starch, or complex carbohydrates, which are a vital part of a healthy diet. Starchy foods, such as cereals or edible grains (e.g. rice, pasta, bread) and vegetables (particularly root vegetables such as potatoes) form the basis of most vegetarian meals, which is why vegetarianism is generally considered a healthy option. Complex carbo-

hydrates usually come complete with fibre, vitamins and minerals.

VITAMINS
Vitamins perform many roles: some help release energy from other foods as we digest them or are needed in combination with other nutrients; some promote healthy eyes, skin, hair, nervous system and other tissues; others help prevent disease. The fat-soluble vitamins A, D, E and K can be stored in the body, but the water-soluble vitamin C and the many vitamins in the B group cannot be stored, and must be regularly taken in from food. A balanced vegetarian diet supplies most of these vitamins, but vegans may need to supplement their intake of B12, found in animal products such as milk, cheese and eggs.

MINERALS
Minerals have many vital functions. They cannot be made by the body and must be provided by foods. Most minerals are available from a varied diet, but vegetarians and vegans may need to supplement their intake of calcium, iron and zinc. Calcium is necessary for healthy bones, tissues and teeth and is found in dairy products, dark green vegetables, including watercress and parsley, wheat, dried fruits and nuts.

Iron is needed for healthy blood and can be found in green vegetables, pulses, nuts, some cereals and some dried fruits. Zinc helps the body's healing and regrowth of cells; it is present in nuts, beans and cereals. Iron and zinc obtained from vegetable rather than animal foods are harder for the body to absorb, but taking vitamin C at the same time helps absorption.

FATS

Fats are needed by a healthy body, but in such small proportions that deficiencies are quite unlikely. Saturated fats – found in animal products (eggs, butter, cream, milk, cheese) – raise the cholesterol in the blood and may lead to coronary heart disease. Unsaturated fats – vegetable oils such as sunflower and olive oil – may actually help lower cholesterol levels, and should be used instead of butter whenever possible.

GLOSSARY OF INGREDIENTS

STORE CUPBOARD

Balsamic vinegar Italian vinegar that has been aged for anything up to 20 years in oak casks (much like some red wines). It is dark, with an intense, slightly sweet flavour.

Buckwheat Small triangular-shaped grain, available plain, roasted or milled into flour. The roasted variety has a deeper flavour. Sometimes called kasha, it is a staple food of Russia and Eastern Europe and is served as an accompaniment.

Bulgar wheat Cracked wheat that has been partially processed. Sometimes sold as cracked wheat or pourgouri, it is used extensively in Middle Eastern cooking where it is eaten in the same way as rice.

Capers Small buds of a flowering shrub grown in the Mediterranean region. Normally pickled in brine or salted, they should be washed and dried before use.

Cassis A fruit liqueur or syrup made from blackcurrants; usually added to wine or Champagne to serve as a refreshing aperitif.

Chilli sauce This can be found in many supermarkets and Oriental stores. To make your own version, put 1 tablespoon of soft brown sugar in a small saucepan with 2 tablespoons of dark soy sauce, 1 tablespoon of lime juice and 1 red chilli, deseeded and chopped finely. Heat gently until the sugar dissolves.

Coconut milk This is available in cans from ethnic stores or larger supermarkets. Alternatively, blocks of creamed coconut can be dissolved in hot water. Once opened, creamed coconut should be removed from the can and stored in the refrigerator.

Couscous Actually a type of pasta, although it is generally treated like a grain and is pre-soaked before cooking to soften it. Used in North African and Middle Eastern cooking.

Curry paste Mild, medium and hot versions are widely available, usually sold in jars.

Dried ceps Dried mushrooms that need reconstituting in boiling water for at least 20 minutes before use (the soaking water is often used in the recipe). Also known as *porcini*, their Italian name. Dried ceps are available from specialist food stores and delicatessens. They have an intense flavour, so only a few are needed.

Dulse seaweed Available dried from health food stores, this dark purple red seaweed has a strong flavour and is similar to Japanese *nori*.

Fermented black beans Tiny black beans with a strong flavour, available in both packets and cans from Oriental stores. The beans should be soaked in cold water for 30 minutes before use, to remove excess saltiness.

Garam masala A ready-made powder made up of a blend of several different Indian spices.

Kalamata olives Purple-brown Greek olives with a pointed end.

Millet A small pinhead grain with a nutty flavour. Needs no soaking if it is to be cooked through.

Nuts Should be bought in small quantities and used as quickly as possible as they do not keep well.

Oils Olive oil should be extra virgin unless the recipe states otherwise. Use sunflower oil or a good quality vegetable oil for deep-frying. Nut oils do not keep well and should be stored in a cool dark place.

Passata Sieved tomatoes, available from supermarkets.

Pasta and noodles Italian pasta is available fresh or dried, in hundreds of shapes and sizes. Making your own pasta (see page 24) will allow you to produce ravioli with delicious vegetar-

Making ravioli

1 Put a heaped teaspoonful of filling per ravioli parcel on the sheet of pasta.

2 Lay a second sheet of pasta over the top and then press down firmly around the mounds of filling.

3 Cut into ravioli rounds with a stamp or into squares with a sharp knife. (See page 25 for a ravioli recipe.)

ian fillings (see picture above). Oriental noodles, usually sold dried, may be made from rice or wheat, sometimes with eggs; they vary from the very fine, threadlike vermicelli to broad, flat noodles.

Polenta The Italian name for corn-meal; used to make a porridge-like gruel or left to set, then grilled, usually in triangular shapes. Quick-cooking polenta is very useful as it takes only a few minutes to cook.

Rice Brown rice contains more nutrients and fibre than white rice and has a nutty flavour. Basmati rice is a slender long-grain brown or white rice which is fragrant in aroma and flavour. Arborio rice is an Italian variety used for making risotto. It is similar in shape and texture to pudding rice, but it never quite softens in the middle.

Rosewater Water flavoured with the essence of rose petals and added to sweet dishes for an exotic flavour. Used mainly in Turkish, Greek and Middle Eastern cooking.

Sun-dried tomatoes Available in dried form or in jars packed in olive or sunflower oil.

Tahini paste A purée of sesame seeds used extensively in Middle Eastern cooking. Oriental sesame paste is different and can be bought from Oriental stores.

Tamari soy sauce This is a slightly thicker, sweeter soy sauce and is available from some supermarkets and Oriental stores.

Yeast Buy fresh yeast if possible when making bread, for a superior flavour. Alternatively use 25 g/1 oz dried yeast or 1 teaspoon fast-action dried yeast instead of 15 g/½ oz fresh yeast. Fast-action dried yeast can be added directly to the flour. It often needs only one rising (see packet instructions) as it contains an enzyme that speeds up the rising process.

FRESH INGREDIENTS

Bouquet garni A bundle of fresh herbs – usually parsley, thyme and bay leaves – used to flavour stocks and stews. They are tied with string or wrapped in muslin so that they can be removed after cooking.

Butternut squash A winter squash, but it is often available all year round. It has a smooth, thick, pale orange skin and is club-shaped.

Celeriac A root vegetable with greenish knobbly skin. Its flavour is similar to celery and it has a creamy texture once cooked.

Coriander Fresh coriander is a popular herb throughout the Middle East, Asia and South America. The roots that are still attached to bunches of coriander are used as an aromatic in Thai cooking.

Fennel The fennel bulb has an aniseed-like flavour and is eaten raw in salads or cooked. The feathery fronds are used as a herb or garnish. Dill is a suitable alternative to the fronds.

Jerusalem artichoke A tuber, unrelated to the globe artichoke. Small and knobbly with a beige skin, Jerusalem artichoke has a delicious, nutty, slightly peppery flavour, and is excellent in soups, stews or roasted as a vegetable.

Kaffir lime leaves A variety of lime leaf used in Far Eastern cooking and available fresh, frozen or dried from supermarkets and Oriental stores.

Lemon grass A fibrous broad-leaved grass from South-East Asia which imparts an aromatic lemon flavour and is usually discarded before serving. Lemon grass is used in Far Eastern cooking and is available fresh, dried and powdered from supermarkets and Oriental stores.

Tomatoes Deep red tomatoes with a firm texture are best. Cherry tomatoes can be red, orange or yellow and have a sweet flavour. Plum tomatoes are an Italian variety, good for cooking and available canned.

DAIRY AND CHILLED INGREDIENTS

Cheese Vegetarians should always look for the 'V' symbol on cheese to ensure that it is made with vegetable rennet. Cheddar, Cheshire, Red Leicester, dolcelatte, feta and many goats' cheeses are widely available as suitable for vegetarians.

Crème fraîche A French lightly soured cream, similar in taste to our soured cream.

Egg glaze To make an effective glaze for pastry, beat 1 egg until completely smooth, then beat in 2 tablespoons water or milk and a pinch of salt.

Filo pastry Paper-thin sheets of pastry used in Greek, Turkish and Middle Eastern cooking. Available both fresh and frozen in various sheet sizes.

Fromage frais A fresh curd cheese made from cows' milk. It has a similar texture to thick yogurt and can be used as a low-fat alternative to cream.

Mascarpone An Italian full-fat cream cheese made from cows' milk.

Mozzarella An Italian full-fat fresh cheese used for salads and pizzas. Buffaloes' milk mozzarella has a better texture and flavour, although it is more expensive than cows' milk mozzarella.

Olive paste Widely available, but check the ingredients list as not all are suitable for vegetarians. To make your own, put 125 g/4 oz pitted black olives, 15 g/½ oz basil leaves and 15 g/½ oz drained capers in a liquidizer with 4 tablespoons extra virgin olive oil and process to make a smooth paste.

Pastry Frozen and chilled shortcrust pastry are widely available, but making your own produces a far superior flavour. Recipes for shortcrust, flaky and suet pastries are given in the chapter beginning on page 56. Flaky pastry has a wonderful, light texture, similar to puff pastry; it is a little tricky to make, so the folding and rolling steps are shown in the picture below.

Ricotta An Italian fresh cheese with a mild taste and light texture. Suitable for both sweet and savoury dishes, and often associated with stuffed pasta dishes and gnocchi. If unavailable, curd cheese can be substituted.

Vegetable suet A suet made from palm and sunflower oils which is suitable for vegetarians.

MAKING FLAKY PASTRY
(See page 61 for the basic recipe.)
1 Dot the butter over ⅔ of the dough.

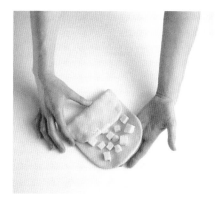

2 Fold the uncovered third of dough over the covered dough and the remaining dough back over that.

3 Seal the edges firmly with a rolling pin, turn the dough once to the left and roll out to an oblong.

Soups and Starters

Oven-baked Soup

1 onion, chopped roughly

2 whole garlic cloves

1 kg/2 lb root vegetables (carrots, leeks, parsnips, swede), chopped roughly

4 tablespoons extra virgin olive oil

2 teaspoons clear honey

4 thyme sprigs

4 rosemary sprigs

2 bay leaves

4 ripe tomatoes, quartered

1.2 litres/2 pints Vegetable Stock (see page 94)

salt and pepper

TO SERVE:

French bread, toasted

Garlic Sauce (see page 76)

1 Toss the onion, garlic and root vegetables with the oil and honey, place in a pan. Add the herbs and place in a preheated oven, 200°C (400°F), Gas Mark 6, for 25 minutes. Add the tomatoes and roast for 25 minutes. Reduce the temperature to 190°C (375°F), Gas Mark 5.

2 Discard the herbs and put the vegetables into a liquidizer. Add half the stock and process until smooth. Blend in the remaining stock. Transfer to a casserole, season to taste and bake for 20 minutes. Serve with toasted French bread and garlic sauce.

Serves 4

Preparation time: 15 minutes

Cooking time: 1¼ hours

Oven temperature: 200°C (400°F), Gas Mark 6, then 190°C (375°F), Gas Mark 5

Fava

This puréed bean paste is similar to hummus, but is made with yellow split peas. It is a Greek dish, served as a dip as part of a meze (selection of little appetizers).

- 50 g/2 oz yellow split peas, rinsed
- 4 tablespoons extra virgin olive oil
- 1 small garlic clove, crushed
- 1 tablespoon lemon juice
- ¼ teaspoon ground cumin
- ½ teaspoon mustard powder
- pinch of cayenne pepper

- salt and pepper

TO GARNISH:

- 1 tablespoon chopped fresh parsley
- 1 tablespoon chopped red pepper
- pinch of cayenne pepper
- 1 tablespoon extra virgin olive oil

1 Put the split peas in a saucepan and add enough cold water to cover the peas by about 2.5 cm/1 inch. Bring to the boil and simmer over a low heat, stirring frequently, for 30–35 minutes until all the water is absorbed and the peas are cooked. Leave to cool slightly.

2 Place the peas in a liquidizer with all the remaining ingredients, season to taste, and process until smooth, adding 2–3 tablespoons of boiling water if the mixture is too thick.
3 Transfer to a serving dish and sprinkle with the parsley, pepper and cayenne. Drizzle over the olive oil. Serve with a selection of prepared raw vegetables and warm pitta bread for dipping.

Serves 4
Preparation time: 5 minutes
Cooking time: 40–45 minutes

Caldo Verde and Smoked Tofu Soup

Caldo verde is a traditional Spanish soup of cabbage, beans and bacon. Smoked tofu makes a nutritious and tasty substitute for the bacon.

- 125 g/4 oz dried cannellini beans, soaked overnight
- 1 small onion, chopped roughly
- 4 whole garlic cloves
- 250 g/8 oz smoked tofu (bean curd), cubed
- 2 tablespoons extra virgin olive oil
- 1 small potato, cubed
- 1 tablespoon chopped fresh sage
- 175 g/6 oz Savoy cabbage, shredded roughly
- 300 ml/½ pint Vegetable Stock (see page 94)
- salt and pepper

1 Drain the soaked beans, rinse and place in a large saucepan. Add 1.2 litres/2 pints water, bring to the boil and boil rapidly for 10 minutes, then reduce the heat and simmer gently for 45 minutes.
2 Meanwhile, toss the onion, garlic and tofu in half the oil and place in a roasting pan. Place in a preheated oven, 200°C (400°F), Gas Mark 6, for 35 minutes, turning occasionally until golden.
3 Heat the remaining oil in a large saucepan, add the potato and sage and fry for 10 minutes until browned.

Stir into the beans with the roasted vegetables and tofu, cabbage, stock and seasoning. Bring to the boil, cover and simmer gently for 20 minutes until the potatoes and cabbage are cooked. Serve hot, with warm bread.

Serves 4–6
Preparation time: 20 minutes, plus overnight soaking
Cooking time: 1¼ hours
Oven temperature: 200°C (400°F), Gas Mark 6

Green Bean and Vegetable Soup with Pesto

This wonderfully aromatic soup is a classic from the south of France, where it is known as soupe au pistou. It is served with fragrant pesto sauce, which is spooned into the soup as it is served.

- 2 tablespoons extra virgin olive oil
- 1 leek, sliced
- 2 garlic cloves, crushed
- 1 potato, diced
- 1 celery stick, sliced
- 1 tablespoon chopped fresh thyme
- 1 x 425 g/14 oz can flageolet beans
- 600 ml/1 pint Vegetable Stock (see page 94)
- 1 courgette, diced
- 50 g/2 oz French beans, halved
- 125 g/4 oz frozen broad beans, thawed
- 1 quantity Pesto Sauce (see page 95)
- salt and pepper

TO SERVE:

- French bread
- freshly grated vegetarian Parmesan cheese (optional)

1 Heat the oil in a large saucepan and fry the leek and garlic for 5 minutes. Add the potato, celery and thyme and fry for a further 10 minutes until light golden.
2 Stir in the flageolet beans with their liquid and the vegetable stock, return to the boil, cover and simmer gently for a further 20 minutes. Add the courgette, French beans and broad beans and cook for a further 10 minutes. Add seasoning to taste.
3 Serve the soup in large bowls. Stir in a spoonful of pesto and serve at once with crusty French bread and grated cheese, if wished.

Serves 4
Preparation time: 15 minutes
Cooking time: 35–40 minutes

Chick Pea, Pasta and Spinach Soup

- 2 tablespoons extra virgin olive oil
- 2 garlic cloves, crushed
- 1 onion, chopped
- 1 tablespoon chopped fresh rosemary
- 2 x 425 g/14 oz cans chick peas
- 1.2 litres/2 pints Vegetable Stock (see page 94)
- 75 g/3 oz small pasta shapes
- 125 g/4 oz fresh spinach leaves, shredded
- salt and pepper

TO SERVE:
- freshly grated nutmeg
- croûtons (see right)
- freshly grated vegetarian Parmesan cheese

1 Heat the oil in a large saucepan and fry the garlic, onion and rosemary over a low heat for 5 minutes until softened but not golden. Add the chick peas with their liquid and the vegetable stock, bring to the boil, cover and simmer for 30 minutes.

2 Add the pasta, return to the boil and simmer for 6–8 minutes.

3 Stir in the spinach and continue cooking for a further 5 minutes until both the pasta and spinach are tender. Season to taste and serve at once, sprinkled with nutmeg, croûtons and grated Parmesan.

Serves 6

Preparation time: 10 minutes
Cooking time: 45 minutes

Croûtons

Remove the crusts from 4 thick slices of one day-old white bread. Cut all of the bread into cubes. Heat 4 tablespoons of olive oil in a frying pan. When the oil is hot, add the bread and stir-fry for 2–3 minutes until the bread cubes are golden and crisp on all sides and all the way through. Remove the croûtons from the frying pan with a slotted spoon and then drain thoroughly on paper towels in order to remove any excess oil there may still be. Use the croûtons as desired.

Serves 6

Preparation time: 2 minutes
Cooking time: 2–3 minutes

Smoky Sweetcorn Soup with Lime Butter

- 4 sweetcorn cobs, about 250 g/8 oz each
- 4 tablespoons extra virgin olive oil
- 1 onion, chopped
- 2 garlic cloves, chopped
- 250 g/8 oz potato, chopped
- 900 ml/1½ pints Vegetable Stock (see page 94)
- 300 ml/½ pint milk, warmed
- pinch of cayenne pepper
- salt and pepper

LIME BUTTER:

- 125 g/4 oz butter
- grated rind and juice of 1 lime
- 2 tablespoons chopped fresh coriander

1 First make the lime butter. In a small bowl beat together the butter, lime rind and juice and the coriander until evenly combined. Add a little salt and pepper to taste and roll into a log shape. Wrap in foil and refrigerate until required.

2 Strip away the outer leaves of the corn, brush each cob with oil and sprinkle with salt and pepper. Grill for 15 minutes, turning frequently until charred on all sides. Remove from the heat and leave to cool slightly.

3 Heat the remaining oil in a saucepan and fry the onion and garlic for 5 minutes until softened, then add the potato and fry for a further 5 minutes.

4 Hold the corn cobs vertically and cut downwards to remove the kernels; add to the saucepan with the stock and milk. Bring to the boil, cover and simmer gently for 30 minutes. Transfer to a liquidizer and process until the soup is smooth.

5 Return the soup to the pan, add the cayenne and salt and pepper and heat through gently. Serve hot, garnished with thin slices of lime butter.

Serves 6–8
Preparation time: 15 minutes
Cooking time: 45 minutes

VARIATION

Roasted Sweetcorn with Lime Butter

Peel open the leaves of the corn, spread the kernels with lime butter, then wrap the leaves back over the cobs. Reserve any remaining butter. Brush the outer leaves with oil and place in an ovenproof dish in a preheated oven, 230°C (450°F), Gas Mark 8, for 30 minutes until tender. Serve hot, with the remaining butter.

Serves 4
Preparation time: 15 minutes
Cooking time: 30 minutes
Oven temperature: 230°C (450°F), Gas Mark 8

Mexican Soup with Avocado Salsa

- 2 tablespoons sunflower oil
- 1 large onion, chopped
- 2 garlic cloves, crushed
- 2 teaspoons ground coriander
- 1 teaspoon ground cumin
- 1 red pepper, cored, deseeded and diced
- 2 red chillies, deseeded and chopped
- 1 x 425 g/14 oz can red kidney beans
- 750 ml/1¼ pints tomato juice
- 1–2 tablespoons chilli sauce (to taste)
- 25 g/1 oz tortilla chips, crushed, plus extra to garnish

AVOCADO SALSA:

- 1 small ripe avocado
- 4 spring onions, chopped finely
- 1 tablespoon lemon juice
- 1 tablespoon chopped fresh coriander
- salt and pepper

1 Heat the oil in a large saucepan, add the onion, garlic, spices, pepper and chillies and fry gently for 10 minutes. Add all the remaining ingredients except the tortilla chips, bring to the boil, cover and simmer gently for 30 minutes.

2 Meanwhile, make the avocado salsa. Peel, stone and finely dice the avocado and combine with the remaining ingredients, season to taste, cover and set aside.

3 Process all the soup in a liquidizer, together with the tortilla chips. Return the soup to a clean saucepan, season to taste and heat through. Serve the soup at once with the avocado salsa, garnished with some extra tortilla chips.

Serves 6
Preparation time: 30 minutes
Cooking time: 45 minutes

Leek and Filo Parcels

These filo parcels make an elegant dinner party starter.

- 40 g/1½ oz butter
- 500 g/1 lb leeks, sliced thinly
- 1 garlic clove, crushed
- 4 tablespoons crème fraîche or fromage frais, plus extra to serve
- 1 tablespoon chopped fresh chervil
- freshly grated nutmeg
- 25 g/1 oz fresh white breadcrumbs
- 25 g/1 oz vegetarian Parmesan cheese, grated
- 8 large sheets filo pastry, thawed if frozen
- extra virgin olive oil, for brushing
- salt and pepper
- chervil sprigs, to garnish

1 Melt half the butter in a frying pan, add the leeks and garlic and fry gently for 4–5 minutes until the leeks are tender. Leave to cool slightly and then stir in the crème fraîche or fromage frais, chervil, nutmeg and season with salt and pepper.

2 Melt the remaining butter in another pan, add the breadcrumbs and stir-fry for 4–5 minutes until golden. Stir into the leek mixture with the Parmesan.

3 Cut each sheet of pastry length-ways into 3 strips. Brush one strip with oil, place a second on top and brush again (keep the remaining sheets covered with a damp tea towel as you work, to prevent the pastry from drying out).

4 Place a heaped tablespoonful of the leek mixture at one end of the filo pastry. Fold over on the diagonal and continue folding along the length of the pastry to enclose the filling. Brush with oil and transfer to an oiled baking sheet. Repeat to make 12 triangles.

5 Place in a preheated oven, 200°C (400°F), Gas Mark 6, for 20–25 minutes until golden. Serve with extra crème fraîche. Garnish with chervil.

Serves 4–6

Preparation time: 15 minutes
Cooking time: 30–35 minutes
Oven temperature: 200°C (400°F), Gas Mark 6

Bruschetta

- 4 thick slices of day-old rustic-style bread
- 2 garlic cloves, halved
- extra virgin olive oil, to drizzle

1 Toast the bread lightly on both sides, either over a barbecue or under a hot grill. Immediately rub the toast all over with the garlic cloves and drizzle with as much olive oil as liked. Either serve at once or add one of the suggested toppings.

Serves 4
Preparation time: 2 minutes
Cooking time: 3–4 minutes

Grilled Tomato and Olive Paste Topping

- 4 firm ripe plum tomatoes, quartered
- extra virgin olive oil
- 2 tablespoons Olive Paste (see page 9)
- basil leaves, shredded if large
- salt and pepper

1 Place the tomatoes in a roasting pan with a little oil and place under a preheated hot grill for 10 minutes until tender and golden.
2 Just before serving, prepare the bruschetta.

3 Spread the olive paste over one side of each bruschetta and top with the grilled tomatoes, basil leaves and salt and pepper. Serve at once.

Serves 4
Preparation time: 5 minutes, plus making bruschetta and olive paste
Cooking time: 14 minutes

Aubergine and Cumin Topping

- 1 tablespoon cumin seeds
- 75 ml/3 fl oz extra virgin olive oil
- 1 teaspoon grated lemon rind
- 2 small aubergines, sliced
- 125 g/4 oz rocket leaves
- 1 tablespoon French Dressing (see page 95)

1 Dry-fry the cumin seeds in a small frying pan until they start to pop and give off a smoky aroma. Carefully add the oil and lemon rind, remove from the heat and leave to infuse for several hours. Strain the oil into a bowl and reserve.
2 Trim the aubergines and cut each one lengthways into 4 thick slices. Brush lightly with the cumin-scented oil and place under a preheated hot grill. Cook for 6–8 minutes until charred, turn over and repeat. Leave to cool to room temperature.
3 Just before serving, prepare the bruschetta. Top with the aubergine slices and drizzle over a little of the cumin-scented oil.
4 Toss the rocket leaves with the French dressing, arrange over the aubergines and drizzle over the remaining cumin oil. Serve at once.

Serves 4
Preparation time: 5 minutes, plus infusing time and making bruschetta and dressing
Cooking time: 18–20 minutes

Wild and Cultivated Mushroom Topping

- 15 g/½ oz dried ceps
- 100 ml/3½ fl oz boiling water
- 2 tablespoons extra virgin olive oil
- 1 garlic clove, crushed
- 375 g/12 oz mixed cultivated mushrooms, sliced
- 1 tablespoon chopped fresh thyme
- 1 tablespoon chopped fresh parsley
- freshly grated vegetarian Parmesan cheese
- salt and pepper

1 Soak the ceps in the boiling water for 20 minutes, then drain, reserving the liquid. Slice the ceps.
2 Heat the oil in a frying pan, add the garlic, ceps, sliced mushrooms and thyme and stir-fry for 3–4 minutes until golden. Add the reserved cep liquid, cover and cook over a low heat for 5 minutes.
3 Meanwhile, prepare the bruschetta. Spoon on the mushroom mixture and top with the parsley, Parmesan and salt and pepper. Serve the topped bruschetta at once.

Serves 4
Preparation time: 10 minutes, plus 20 minutes soaking and making bruschetta
Cooking time: 10 minutes

Escarole and Grilled Pepper Topping

- 1 red pepper, cored, deseeded and quartered
- 1 yellow pepper, cored, deseeded and quartered
- 2 tablespoons hazelnut oil
- 2 garlic cloves, sliced
- 1 tablespoon grated lemon rind
- 25 g/1 oz sultanas
- 25 g/1 oz flaked hazelnuts
- 175 g/6 oz escarole, shredded
- salt and pepper

1 Place the pepper quarters under a preheated hot grill for 6–8 minutes on each side until charred and tender. Transfer to a plastic bag and set aside until cool enough to handle. Peel off the skin and slice the flesh.
2 Heat the hazelnut oil in a frying pan, add the garlic, lemon rind, sultanas and hazelnuts and fry gently for 5 minutes until golden. Add the escarole and cook over a low heat for 5 minutes until tender.
3 Meanwhile, prepare the bruschetta. Divide the escarole mixture between the bruschetta and top with the grilled peppers and salt and pepper. Serve at once.

Serves 4
Preparation time: 15 minutes, plus making bruschetta
Cooking time: 18–20 minutes

Pasta and Noodles

Baked Pasta with Aubergine and Pepper

4 tablespoons extra virgin olive oil

1 large aubergine, diced

1 onion, chopped

2 red peppers, cored, deseeded and diced

1 tablespoon dried oregano

175 g/6 oz dried penne pasta

1 quantity Fresh Tomato Sauce (see page 94)

2 egg yolks

250 g/8 oz crème fraîche or fromage frais

2 tablespoons milk

125 g/4 oz vegetarian feta cheese, diced

salt and pepper

1 Heat half the oil in a large frying pan, add the aubergine and stir-fry over a medium heat for 6–8 minutes until golden and tender. Remove with a slotted spoon. Add the remaining oil and fry the onion, peppers and oregano for 10 minutes.

2 Cook the pasta according to the packet instructions. Drain well and immediately toss with the tomato sauce and vegetables, seasoning to taste. Spoon into a deep, oiled, 20 x 30 cm/8 x 12 inch baking dish.

3 Beat together the remaining ingredients and pour over the pasta mixture. Place in a preheated oven, 180°C (350°F), Gas Mark 4, for 35–40 minutes until the topping is set and golden. Leave to stand for 5 minutes, then serve with a mixed salad.

Serves 4–6

Preparation time: 15 minutes, plus making sauce

Cooking time: 50 minutes

Oven temperature: 180°C (350°F), Gas Mark 4

Fresh Pasta

Making fresh pasta is much easier with the aid of a pasta machine – well worth buying if you love pasta. The first time you make the pasta sheets, take them to the second thinnest setting on the machine and then progress to the thinnest when you feel more confident. Pasta flour, made from durum (hard) wheat, is available from some supermarkets and Italian delicatessens. Strong white bread flour is the closest alternative, and is easier to use.

- 250 g/8 oz pasta flour or strong white bread flour, plus extra for dusting
- 3 teaspoons salt
- 2 eggs, plus 1 egg yolk
- 1 tablespoon extra virgin olive oil
- 1–2 tablespoons cold water
- 1 quantity Pesto Sauce (see page 95) or ½ quantity Fresh Tomato Sauce (see page 94)

1 Sift the flour and 1 teaspoon salt into a bowl, make a well in the centre and gradually work in the eggs, egg yolk, oil and enough water to form a soft dough.
2 Turn out on to a lightly floured surface and knead for 5 minutes until the dough is smooth and elastic. Brush with a little oil, cover and leave to rest for 30 minutes.
3 Divide the dough into 8 pieces. Take one piece and pat into a flattish rectangle. With the pasta rolling machine set at its widest setting, feed the dough through twice.

Repeat the process at each setting, feeding the sheet of dough through the rollers lengthways, until the sheet is long and very thin. Cut the sheet in half widthways and hang over a pole to dry for 5 minutes.
4 Repeat with the remaining pieces of dough to make 16 sheets of pasta. Pass each sheet through either the tagliatelle or linguine cutter of the machine, then hang the noodles over the pole to dry for a further 5 minutes. Taking about 12 noodles at a time, wind them into 'nests' and place on a floured tea towel.
5 Bring a large saucepan of water

(at least 3.5 litres/6 pints) to a rolling boil. Add 2 teaspoons of salt and as soon as the water boils again drop in the pasta 'nests'. Return to the boil and cook for 2–3 minutes until the pasta is al dente.
6 Drain the pasta, return to the pan, toss in a sauce of your choice and serve at once.

Serves 4 as a main course or 6 as a starter
Preparation time: 20 minutes, plus 40 minutes resting
Cooking time: 2–3 minutes

Beetroot Ravioli with Dill Cream

- 1 quantity Fresh Pasta (see left)

FILLING:
- 1 tablespoon extra virgin olive oil
- 1 small onion, chopped finely
- ½ teaspoon caraway seeds
- 175 g/6 oz cooked beetroot, chopped
- 175 g/6 oz ricotta or curd cheese
- 25 g/1 oz homemade dried breadcrumbs
- 1 egg yolk
- 2 tablespoons freshly grated vegetarian Parmesan cheese
- grated nutmeg
- salt and pepper

DILL CREAM:
- 4 tablespoons walnut oil
- 4 tablespoons chopped fresh dill
- 1 tablespoon drained green peppercorns in brine, crushed
- 6 tablespoons crème fraîche or fromage frais

1 Make the pasta dough, following steps 1 and 2 of the recipe, see left. Wrap in clingfilm and leave to rest.

2 For the filling, heat the oil in a frying pan, add the onion and caraway seeds and fry over a medium heat for 5 minutes until light golden. Add the beetroot and cook for a further 5 minutes.

3 Process the beetroot mixture in a liquidizer until smooth; leave to cool. Beat in the ricotta or curd cheese, breadcrumbs, egg yolk, Parmesan and nutmeg. Season to taste.

4 Following step 3 of the pasta recipe, roll out the dough to form 8 sheets; cut each in half widthways. Lay one sheet on a floured surface and place 5 heaped teaspoons of the filling at 2.5 cm/1 inch intervals over the dough (see page 8).

5 Dampen around the mounds of filling with a wet pastry brush and lay a second sheet of pasta over the top; press around the mounds to seal well. Cut into round ravioli using a cutter or into squares using a sharp knife and place on a floured tea towel. Repeat to make 40 ravioli.

6 Bring a large saucepan of water to a rolling boil and add 2 teaspoons of salt. Drop the ravioli into the boiling water, return to the boil and cook for 3–4 minutes until al dente.

7 Meanwhile, make the dill cream. Heat the oil in a small saucepan, add the chopped dill and green peppercorns and remove from the heat. Stir in the crème fraîche.

8 Drain the ravioli well, transfer to a warm serving dish and toss with the dill cream. Serve at once.

Serves 4–6
Preparation time: 1 hour, including making pasta
Cooking time: 22–25 minutes

Courgette and Red Pesto Pasta

- 375 g/12 oz dried pasta shapes
- 6 tablespoons extra virgin olive oil
- 2 garlic cloves, sliced
- 1 teaspoon grated lemon rind
- 1 dried red chilli, deseeded and crushed
- 500 g/1 lb courgettes, sliced thinly
- 1 tablespoon shredded basil leaves
- 2–3 tablespoons Red Pesto (see page 95)
- pepper

1 Cook the pasta according to the packet instructions.
2 Meanwhile, heat 2 tablespoons of the oil in a deep frying pan, add the garlic, lemon rind and chilli and fry for 2–3 minutes until just golden. Add the courgettes and basil and stir-fry for a further 3–4 minutes, until the courgettes are golden.
3 Drain the cooked pasta thoroughly and add to the courgette pan with the remaining oil, red pesto and plenty of freshly ground black pepper. Toss well over a low heat for 1 minute and serve at once.

Serves 4
Preparation time: 10 minutes
Cooking time: 12–15 minutes

VARIATION

Pasta with Lettuce and Peas

- 375 g/12 oz dried pasta
- 6 tablespoons hazelnut or extra virgin olive oil
- 1 leek, sliced thinly
- 2 garlic cloves, chopped
- 2 teaspoons grated lime rind
- 2 little gem lettuces, shredded roughly
- 250 g/8 oz frozen peas
- 4 tablespoons chopped fresh chives
- 2 tablespoons lime juice
- 4 tablespoons soured cream
- salt and pepper

1 Cook the pasta according to the packet instructions.
2 Meanwhile, heat half the oil in a deep frying pan, add the leek, garlic and lime rind and fry gently for 3 minutes. Add the lettuce, peas, chives and lime juice, cover and cook over a low heat for about 4–5 minutes until the lettuce and peas are cooked.
3 Drain the cooked pasta thoroughly, toss with the remaining oil and the soured cream, season to taste with salt and pepper and stir into the lettuce mixture. Serve at once.

Serves 4
Preparation time: 10 minutes
Cooking time: 12–15 minutes

Hot and Sour Thai Noodles

This delicious, fresh-tasting salad uses thin rice vermicelli noodles; thin egg noodles are an alternative. Although this dish can be served at once when it is still warm, the flavours improve if it is left to cool to room temperature.

- 2 tablespoons sunflower oil
- 1 teaspoon sesame oil
- 2 garlic cloves, crushed
- 1 teaspoon chilli flakes
- 2 carrots, cut into matchsticks
- 50 g/2 oz small broccoli florets
- 50 g/2 oz small cauliflower florets
- 125 g/4 oz snap peas
- 125 g/4 oz shiitake mushrooms, sliced
- 125 g/4 oz Chinese cabbage, shredded
- 125 g/4 oz bean sprouts
- 75 g/3 oz rice vermicelli
- 50 g/2 oz cashew nuts

DRESSING:

- 2½ tablespoons sunflower oil
- 1 tablespoon caster sugar
- 2 tablespoons lime juice
- 1 tablespoon rice or wine vinegar
- 1 tablespoon fish or light soy sauce
- 1 teaspoon Tabasco sauce
- 1 tablespoon each chopped fresh coriander and mint
- salt and pepper

1 Heat the sunflower and sesame oils in a small saucepan with the garlic and chilli flakes until the oil starts to smoke. Carefully strain the oil into a wok or large frying pan.

2 Reheat the oil and when hot add the carrots, broccoli, cauliflower, peas and mushrooms. Stir-fry for 2 minutes, then add the cabbage and bean sprouts and stir-fry for a further 2 minutes until the vegetables are just wilted. Remove from the heat.
3 Soak the noodles according to the packet instructions. In a small bowl whisk all the dressing ingredients together and season to taste. Drain the noodles and toss with a little of the dressing.
4 Stir the remaining dressing into the vegetables. Spoon the noodles on to individual plates and top with the vegetables and nuts; serve at once. Alternatively, arrange the noodles on a large plate, top with the vegetables and leave to cool for up to 1 hour. Sprinkle over the nuts just before serving.

Serves 4
Preparation time: 15 minutes
Cooking time: 5 minutes

VARIATION

Crispy Thai Noodles

Prepare and cook the vegetables as above and toss with all the dressing. Replace the vermicelli noodles with thin egg noodles and soak according to the packet instructions. Drain and dry thoroughly on paper towels.

Just before serving, heat about 10 cm/4 inches vegetable oil in a heavy-bottomed saucepan to

180–190ºC (350–375ºF), or until a cube of bread browns in 30 seconds.

Add the noodles in batches and fry for 1 minute until crisp. Drain on paper towels. Serve the vegetable salad topped with the crispy noodles.

Potato Gnocchi with Fennel Sauce

Gnocchi are little dumplings, sometimes made with flour or semolina, sometimes with potatoes or other vegetables. These potato dumplings will be lighter if the potatoes are mashed and formed into dough while still piping hot (but make sure you wear thick rubber gloves to prevent being scalded). When adding flour to any sort of gnocchi, add only just enough to bind the mixture, forming a dough that is tacky. This will help achieve a light texture in the cooked gnocchi.

Dill can be used if fennel fronds are unavailable.

- 1 kg/2 lb floury potatoes
- 1 egg
- 1 egg yolk
- 175 g/6 oz plain flour
- 1 teaspoon salt
- freshly grated vegetarian Parmesan cheese, to serve

FENNEL SAUCE:
- 4 tablespoons extra virgin olive oil
- 2 tablespoons boiling water
- 1 tablespoon lemon juice
- 2 tablespoons chopped fennel fronds
- salt and pepper
- a few fennel fronds, to garnish

1 Bake the potatoes in a preheated oven, 200°C (400°F), Gas Mark 6, for 1 hour or until tender.
2 Wearing a pair of rubber gloves, peel the potatoes while hot. Lightly mash the potato, and beat in the egg, egg yolk and enough of the flour to form a soft, slightly sticky dough.
3 Bring a large saucepan of lightly salted water to a rolling boil. Roll small pieces of the potato dough in your hands and drop into the boiling water. Cook in batches for 4–5 minutes until they rise to the surface. With a slotted spoon, drain and place in an oiled baking dish. Repeat with the remaining mixture.
4 Whisk all the sauce ingredients together, season to taste and pour over the gnocchi. Heat through in the oven for 6–8 minutes until bubbling and serve at once sprinkled with grated Parmesan and garnished with fennel fronds.

Serves 4
Preparation time: 50 minutes
Cooking time: 1¼ hours
Oven temperature: 200°C (400°F), Gas Mark 6

VARIATION

Mushroom and Tomato Sauce for Gnocchi

- 15 g/½ oz dried ceps
- 150 ml/¼ pint boiling water
- 4 tablespoons extra virgin olive oil
- 2 garlic cloves, crushed
- 4 ripe tomatoes, skinned, deseeded and chopped
- salt and pepper

1 Soak the ceps in the boiling water for 30 minutes, then drain, reserving the liquid. Slice the ceps.
2 Heat the oil in a small saucepan and fry the garlic and ceps for 5 minutes. Add the tomatoes and cep liquid and simmer for a further 5 minutes. Season to taste and keep warm until required.

Makes enough for 4–6 servings of gnocchi
Preparation time: 5 minutes, plus 30 minutes soaking
Cooking time: 10 minutes

Wild Mushroom Lasagne

Unfortunately, fresh wild mushrooms, when available, tend to be very expensive in this country. Dried wild mushrooms or ceps are also expensive, but you will need only a very small quantity. This recipe uses a combination of these and cultivated mushrooms such as oyster and shiitake. These mushrooms are now widely available in most large supermarkets. Of course, if you are a expert mushroom forager and come across an abundance of wild mushrooms, then substitute them for the cultivated variety.

- 15 g/½ oz dried ceps
- 150 ml/¼ pint boiling water
- 3 tablespoons extra virgin olive oil
- 4 shallots, chopped
- 2 garlic cloves, chopped
- 1 tablespoon chopped fresh thyme
- 750 g/1½ lb mixed cultivated mushrooms
- 150 ml/¼ pint dry white wine
- 500 g/1 lb tomatoes, skinned and chopped or 1 x 425 g/14 oz can chopped tomatoes
- 50 g/2 oz drained sun-dried tomatoes in oil, chopped
- 1 tablespoon dark soy sauce
- 12 sheets pre-cooked lasagne or fresh lasagne
- 1 quantity Classic Cheese Sauce (see page 94)
- 250 g/8 oz mozzarella cheese
- salt and pepper

1 Place the dried ceps in a bowl and pour over the boiling water. Leave to soak for 30 minutes, then drain, reserving the liquid. Slice the ceps.
2 Heat the oil in a large frying pan, add the shallots, garlic and thyme and fry for 5 minutes. Add the ceps and fresh mushrooms and stir-fry for 5–6 minutes until golden. Add the wine and boil rapidly for 5 minutes. Stir in the tomatoes, sun-dried tomatoes, reserved cep liquid and soy sauce, bring to the boil and simmer gently for 15 minutes. Season to taste.
3 Assemble the lasagne. Pour one-third of the mushrooms into a 20 x 25 cm/8 x 10 inch lasagne dish and top with 4 sheets of lasagne, one-third of the cheese sauce and one-third of the mozzarella. Repeat with the remaining ingredients, finishing with a layer of cheese sauce and then mozzarella.
4 Place the mushroom lasagne in a preheated oven, 190°C (375°F), Gas Mark 5, for about 45 minutes until bubbling and golden.

Serves 6
Preparation time: 40 minutes, plus 30 minutes soaking, plus making sauce
Cooking time: 40–45 minutes
Oven temperature: 190°C (375°F), Gas Mark 5

Thai Noodles with Vegetables and Tofu

This is a classic, colourful and nutritious noodle dish, similar to many found on Thai menus.

- 250 g/8 oz tofu (bean curd), cubed
- 2 tablespoons dark soy sauce
- 1 teaspoon grated lime rind
- 1.75 litres/3 pints Vegetable Stock (see page 94)
- 2 slices fresh root ginger
- 2 garlic cloves
- 2 coriander sprigs
- 2 stalks lemon grass, crushed
- 1 red chilli, bruised
- 175 g/6 oz dried egg noodles
- 125 g/4 oz shiitake or button mushrooms, sliced
- 2 large carrots, cut into matchsticks
- 125 g/4 oz snap peas
- 125 g/4 oz Chinese cabbage, shredded
- 2 tablespoons chopped fresh coriander
- salt and pepper

1 Put the tofu in a shallow dish with the soy sauce and lime rind and leave to marinate for 30 minutes.
2 Meanwhile, put the vegetable stock into a large saucepan and add the ginger, garlic, coriander sprigs, lemon grass and chilli. Bring the mixture to the boil, reduce the heat, cover the pan and gently simmer the stock for 30 minutes.
3 Strain the cooked vegetable stock into another saucepan, return to the boil and plunge in the noodles. Add the sliced mushrooms and marinated tofu with any remaining marinade. Reduce the heat and simmer gently for 4 minutes.
4 Stir in the carrots, snap peas, shredded Chinese cabbage and the chopped coriander and cook together for a further 3–4 minutes until all the vegetables are just tender. Taste and adjust the seasoning, if necessary. Serve at once.

Serves 4
Preparation time: 20 minutes, plus 30 minutes marinating
Cooking time: 40 minutes

Egg-fried Noodles with Vegetables and Tofu

Many Asian dishes require a fair amount of preparation, but this can often be done well in advance; the last-minute cooking times are always so short that the lengthy preparation is soon forgotten.

- vegetable oil, for deep-frying
- 250 g/8 oz tofu (bean curd), cubed
- 75 g/3 oz dried egg noodles
- 125 g/4 oz broccoli florets
- 125 g/4 oz baby sweetcorn, halved
- 3 tablespoons light soy sauce
- 1 tablespoon lemon juice
- 1 teaspoon sugar
- 1 teaspoon chilli sauce
- 3 tablespoons sunflower oil
- 1 garlic clove, chopped
- 1 red chilli, deseeded and sliced
- 2 eggs, lightly beaten
- 125 g/4 oz drained water chestnuts, sliced

1 In a heavy-bottomed saucepan, heat about 5 cm/2 inches of vegetable oil to 180–190°C (350–375°F), or until a cube of bread browns in 30 seconds. Add the tofu and fry for 3–4 minutes until crisp and lightly golden. Drain the tofu on paper towels.
2 Cook the noodles according to the packet instructions, drain, refresh under cold water and dry well on paper towels.
3 Blanch the broccoli and sweetcorn in a saucepan of boiling water for 1 minute, drain, refresh under cold water and pat dry with paper towels. Mix together the soy sauce, lemon juice, sugar and chilli sauce.
4 Heat the sunflower oil in a wok or large frying pan, add the garlic and chilli and stir-fry for 3 minutes. Add the noodles and stir-fry for 5 minutes until golden and starting to crisp up.

5 Stir in the eggs, and stir-fry for 1 minute, then stir in the sauce mixture, tofu, broccoli, sweetcorn and water chestnuts and stir-fry for a further 2–3 minutes until heated through. Serve at once.

Serves 4
Preparation time: 20 minutes
Cooking time: 10–15 minutes

Rice and Grains

Caribbean Black-eyed Beans and Rice

2 tablespoons sunflower oil

1 small onion, chopped finely

1 garlic clove, crushed

1 teaspoon grated fresh root ginger

½ teaspoon hot paprika

¼ teaspoon ground black pepper

2 tomatoes, skinned and chopped

150 ml/¼ pint coconut milk

250 g/8 oz long-grain rice, rinsed

1 x 425 g/14 oz can black-eyed beans, drained

600 ml/1 pint Vegetable Stock (see page 94)

1 teaspoon salt

a few sprigs of parsley, to garnish

1 Heat the oil in a large saucepan and fry the onion, garlic, ginger, paprika and black pepper for 5 minutes, stirring frequently. Add the tomatoes and coconut milk and simmer gently for 10 minutes.

2 Add the remaining ingredients, bring to the boil, cover and simmer over a low heat for 15 minutes. Remove the saucepan from the heat and leave to stand for 10 minutes. Stir well, taste and adjust the seasoning and serve garnished with the parsley.

Serves 4
Preparation time: 10 minutes
Cooking time: 30 minutes, plus 10 minutes resting

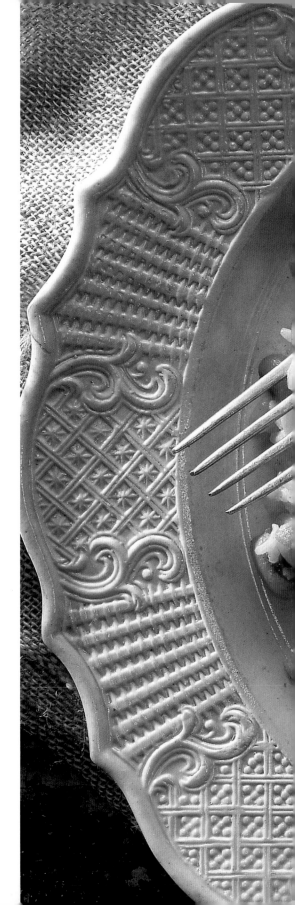

Saffron Millet and Lentils with Radicchio

This colourful and nutritious dish is ideal as an alternative to rice. Puy lentils are often used in French cooking and are particularly nutty in both taste and texture. They are becoming more widely available in this country and can often be found in larger supermarkets.

- pinch of saffron strands
- 900 ml/1½ pints boiling Vegetable Stock (see page 94)
- 125 g/4 oz Puy lentils, rinsed
- 125 g/4 oz millet
- 50 g/2 oz butter
- 1 leek, sliced
- 2 garlic cloves, sliced
- 1 teaspoon ground cinnamon
- 50 g/2 oz currants
- 1 small head radicchio, shredded
- salt and pepper

1 Soak the saffron strands in the boiling vegetable stock for 10 minutes.
2 Put the lentils in a saucepan and add enough water to cover the lentils by about 2.5 cm/1 inch. Bring to the boil, and boil the lentils rapidly for 10 minutes, then drain.
3 Place the millet in a small frying pan and heat gently until the grains start to turn golden.
4 Melt the butter in a saucepan, add the leek, garlic and cinnamon and fry for 3 minutes. Stir in the lentils and millet and then pour in the saffron stock. Bring to the boil, cover and simmer gently for 30 minutes until the lentils and millet are tender.
5 Stir in the currants and shredded radicchio and heat through for 5 minutes. Season to taste with salt and pepper and serve at once.

Serves 4–6
Preparation time: 10 minutes, plus soaking saffron
Cooking time: 50 minutes

Vegetable Biryani

A biryani is an Indian rice dish made with either meat or vegetables, or a combination of both. This method of cooking rice is sure to be rewarded with success every time.

- 250 g/8 oz basmati rice, rinsed
- 6 tablespoons sunflower oil
- 2 large onions, sliced thinly
- 2 garlic cloves, crushed
- 2 teaspoons grated fresh root ginger
- 250 g/8 oz sweet potato, diced
- 2 large carrots, diced
- 1 tablespoon curry paste
- 2 teaspoons ground turmeric
- 1 teaspoon ground cinnamon
- 1 teaspoon chilli powder
- 300 ml/½ pint Vegetable Stock (see page 94)
- 4 ripe tomatoes, skinned, deseeded and diced
- 175 g/6 oz cauliflower florets
- 125 g/4 oz frozen peas, thawed
- 50 g/2 oz cashew nuts, toasted
- 2 tablespoons chopped fresh coriander
- salt and pepper
- 2 hard-boiled eggs, quartered, to serve

1 Bring a large saucepan of salted water to a rolling boil, add the basmati rice and return to a simmer. Cook gently for 5 minutes. Drain, refresh under cold water and drain again. Spread the rice out on a large baking sheet and set aside to dry.
2 Heat 2 tablespoons of the oil in a frying pan, add half the onion and fry over a medium heat for 10 minutes until very crisp and golden. Remove and drain on paper towels. Reserve for garnishing.
3 Add the remaining oil to the pan and fry the remaining onion with the garlic and ginger for 5 minutes. Add the potato, carrots and spices and continue to fry for a further 10 minutes until light golden.
4 Add the vegetable stock and tomatoes, bring to the boil, cover and simmer gently for 20 minutes. Add the cauliflower and peas and cook for a further 8–10 minutes until all the vegetables are tender.
5 Stir in the rice, cashew nuts, coriander and salt and pepper. Cook, stirring, for 3 minutes, then cover and remove from the heat. Leave to stand for 5 minutes before serving. Garnish with the crispy onions and egg quarters.

Serves 4
Preparation time: 25 minutes
Cooking time: 50–55 minutes, plus 5 minutes resting

VARIATION

Gingered Rice with Carrots and Tomatoes

- 250 g/8 oz basmati rice, rinsed
- 4 tablespoons extra virgin olive oil
- 2 garlic cloves, crushed
- 1 tablespoon grated fresh root ginger
- 4 carrots, sliced thinly
- 4 ripe tomatoes, skinned, deseeded and diced
- 2 cinnamon sticks, bruised
- seeds from 3 cardamom pods, bruised
- 1 dried red chilli
- 1 tablespoon lemon juice
- 50 g/2 oz flaked almonds, toasted
- salt and pepper

1 Cook the rice in plenty of boiling, salted water for 5 minutes. Drain, refresh under cold water and drain again. Spread out on a large baking sheet and set aside to dry.
2 Heat the oil in a wok or large frying pan, add the garlic, ginger and carrots and fry for 10 minutes. Add the tomatoes and spices and cook for a further 5 minutes.
3 Stir in the rice, lemon juice, nuts and salt and pepper and stir-fry for 3–4 minutes until the rice is heated through. Serve at once.

Serves 4
Preparation time: 20 minutes
Cooking time: 20 minutes

Baked Buckwheat and Spiced Butter

Don't be put off by the rather dull appearance of this dish. The roasted buckwheat has a fabulous nutty flavour and texture and makes a nice change to rice as a companion dish.

- 75 g/3 oz unsalted butter, softened
- 1 small garlic clove, crushed
- 2 tablespoons chopped fresh coriander
- ¼ teaspoon ground cumin
- ¼ teaspoon ground cinnamon
- pinch of chilli powder
- 250 g/8 oz roasted buckwheat
- 450 ml/¾ pint boiling Vegetable Stock (see page 94)
- sea salt

1 In a small bowl beat together the butter, garlic, coriander and spices until evenly combined. Cover and leave for at least 30 minutes.
2 Use a little of the spiced butter to grease an ovenproof dish. Put in the roasted buckwheat and pour over the boiling stock. Cover with a tight-fitting lid and place in a preheated oven, 200°C (400°F), Gas Mark 6, for 15 minutes.
3 Remove the dish from the oven and leave to stand for 5 minutes. Stir in the remaining spiced butter and sea salt to taste, and serve at once.

Serves 4–6
Preparation time: 10 minutes, plus 30 minutes standing
Cooking time: 15 minutes, plus 5 minutes resting
Oven temperature: 200°C (400°F), Gas Mark 6

VARIATION
Substitute either bulgar wheat or millet for the buckwheat.

Nut and Rice Roast

Nut roasts have the unfortunate reputation of being the epitome of a dull vegetarian meal: a poor substitute for meat. This one is moist, nutty and very tasty, especially when served with onion gravy. It is sure to please even a reluctant vegetarian.

- 15 g/½ oz dried ceps
- 25 g/1 oz butter
- 1 onion, chopped very finely
- 2 celery sticks, chopped very finely
- 1 garlic clove, crushed
- 250 g/8 oz button mushrooms, chopped very finely
- 2 tablespoons chopped fresh parsley
- 1 tablespoon chopped fresh thyme
- 175 g/6 oz cooked brown rice
- 125 g/4 oz each cashew nuts and hazelnuts, toasted and coarsely ground
- 50 g/2 oz walnuts, toasted and coarsely ground
- 125 g/4 oz vegetarian Gruyère or Cheddar cheese, grated
- 1 egg, beaten
- salt and pepper
- a few sprigs of oregano, to garnish
- Onion and Wine Gravy (see page 95), to serve

1 Pour boiling water over the ceps and leave to soak for 30 minutes. Drain and slice the ceps.
2 Melt the butter in a frying pan and fry the onion, celery and garlic for 5 minutes. Stir in the ceps, mushrooms, herbs and rice and fry, stirring frequently, for a further 5 minutes until all the liquid from the mushrooms has evaporated.
3 Transfer the mixture to a large bowl and stir in all the remaining ingredients until evenly combined; season to taste. Press into a greased and base-lined 1 kg/2 lb loaf tin and smooth the surface. Place in a pre-heated oven at 190°C (375°F), Gas Mark 5, for 1–1¼ hours until it feels firm and a skewer inserted into the centre comes out clean.

4 Cover the tin with foil and let the loaf rest for 15 minutes. Turn out and slice. Garnish with oregano and serve hot with onion gravy and vegetables.

Serves 6–8
Preparation time: 30 minutes, plus making gravy
Cooking time: 1½ hours, plus 15 minutes resting
Oven temperature: 190°C (375°F), Gas Mark 5

Barley Bake with Squash, Mushroom and Rosemary

This delicious barley dish resembles a baked risotto in both flavour and texture. The barley never becomes completely tender, giving bite to the dish. Butternut squash is available all year round and is not watery, but has a lovely creamy texture.

- 175 g/6 oz pearl barley
- 600 ml/1 pint boiling Vegetable Stock (see page 94)
- 25 g/1 oz butter, plus extra for greasing
- 1 onion, sliced
- 500 g/1 lb peeled squash, cubed
- 250 g/8 oz shiitake or button mushrooms, halved if large
- 2 tablespoons chopped fresh rosemary
- ½ teaspoon cayenne pepper
- 200 g/7 oz canned chopped tomatoes
- 150 ml/¼ pint single cream
- 50 g/2 oz vegetarian Gruyère or Cheddar cheese, grated
- salt and pepper
- chopped fresh parsley, to garnish

1 Rinse the barley for several minutes under cold running water, drain well and shake dry. Place in a saucepan, pour over the boiling vegetable stock and bring back to the boil. Cover the pan and simmer gently for 40 minutes until the stock is absorbed and the barley is tender.
2 Melt the butter in a frying pan, add the sliced onion and fry gently for 5 minutes, stirring occasionally, until soft but not browned. Add the squash, mushrooms and rosemary to the pan and fry for a further 5 minutes. Stir into the barley with the remaining ingredients, except the parsley, until evenly combined.
3 Transfer the barley mixture to a greased baking dish and place in a preheated oven, 200°C (400°F), Gas Mark 6, for 20 minutes until golden and bubbling. Garnish with some freshly chopped parsley and serve immediately with a mixed salad.

Serves 4–6
Preparation time: 25 minutes
Cooking time: 1 hour
Oven temperature: 200°C (400°F), Gas Mark 6

Beans and Lentils

Mixed Baked Beans

1 x 425 g/14 oz can red kidney beans

1 x 425 g/14 oz can haricot beans

1 x 425 g/14 oz can aduki beans

250 ml/8 fl oz pint passata (sieved tomatoes)

2 tablespoons molasses

½ tablespoon wholegrain mustard

1 tablespoon vegetarian Worcestershire sauce or dark soy sauce

pinch of ground cloves

½ teaspoon salt

1 large onion, chopped finely

2 carrots, diced

2 celery sticks, chopped

2 bay leaves

4 tablespoons chopped fresh parsley

grated vegetarian Cheddar cheese, to serve (optional)

1 Strain the liquid from the beans and pour half into a bowl, discarding the rest. Whisk the passata, molasses, mustard, Worcestershire or soy sauce, cloves and salt into the liquid until evenly combined.

2 Put the beans and all the remaining ingredients, except the parsley, in a casserole and stir in the liquid. Cover with a tight-fitting lid. Place in a preheated oven, 180°C (350°F), Gas Mark 4, for 2 hours. Stir in the parsley and serve, topped with cheese.

Serves 6–8

Preparation time: 15 minutes

Cooking time: 2 hours

Oven temperature: 180°C (350°F), Gas Mark 4

Green Lentil and Vegetable Tagine with Couscous

A tagine is the name of the clay dish in which stews are cooked in many North African countries such as Morocco and Tunisia. The classic accompaniment to a tagine stew is couscous – a type of ground pasta.

- 125 g/4 oz green lentils, rinsed
- 600 ml/1 pint water
- 4 tablespoons extra virgin olive oil
- 2 small onions, cut into wedges
- 2 garlic cloves, chopped
- 1 tablespoon ground coriander
- 2 teaspoons ground cumin
- 1 teaspoon ground turmeric
- 1 teaspoon ground cinnamon
- 12 new potatoes, halved if large
- 2 large carrots, sliced thickly
- 250 g/8 oz couscous
- 2 courgettes, sliced
- 175 g/6 oz button mushrooms
- 300 ml/½ pint tomato juice
- 1 tablespoon tomato purée
- 125 g/4 oz ready-to-eat dried apricots, chopped
- 2 tablespoons chilli sauce, plus extra to serve (optional)

1 Put the lentils in a saucepan with the water. Bring to the boil, cover and simmer for 20 minutes.
2 Meanwhile, heat half the oil in a large saucepan and fry the onions, garlic and spices for 5 minutes. Add the potatoes and carrots and fry for a further 5 minutes. Add the lentils with their cooking liquid, cover and simmer gently for 15 minutes.
3 Rinse the couscous several times under cold running water to moisten all the grains and spread out on a large baking sheet. Sprinkle over a little water and then leave to soak for 15 minutes.
4 Heat the remaining oil in a frying pan and fry the courgettes and mushrooms for 4–5 minutes until lightly golden. Add to the lentil mixture with the tomato juice, tomato purée, dried apricots and chilli sauce and return to the boil. Cook for a further 10 minutes until the vegetables and lentils are tender.
5 Steam the couscous according to the packet instructions or over the stew in a double boiler for 6–7 minutes. Transfer to a large warmed platter, spoon on the vegetable and lentil tagine and serve the juices separately, with extra chilli sauce if liked.

Serves 4–6
Preparation time: 40–45 minutes, plus soaking couscous
Cooking time: 40 minutes

Borlotti Bean Goulash

- 2 tablespoons extra virgin olive oil
- 1 onion, chopped
- 2 carrots, sliced
- 1 teaspoon caraway seeds
- 2 red peppers, cored, deseeded and diced
- 250 g/8 oz sweet potato, cubed
- 2 tablespoons paprika
- 1 teaspoon cayenne pepper
- 600 ml/1 pint Vegetable Stock (see page 94)
- 2 tablespoons tomato purée
- 1 x 425 g/14 oz can borlotti beans, drained

DUMPLINGS:
- 75 g/3 oz self-raising flour
- ½ teaspoon salt
- 50 g/2 oz vegetarian suet
- 15 g/½ oz vegetarian Cheddar cheese, grated
- ½ teaspoon celery salt
- pepper

1 Heat the oil in a large flameproof casserole and add the onion, carrots and caraway seeds. Fry for 5 minutes, then add the peppers, sweet potato, paprika and cayenne and fry for a further 3 minutes.
2 Stir in the stock, tomato purée and drained borlotti beans, bring to the boil, cover and cook over a low heat for 30 minutes.
3 Meanwhile, make the dumplings. Sift the flour and salt into a bowl and stir in the suet, cheese, celery salt and a little pepper. Working quickly and lightly, gradually mix in 4–5 tablespoons of cold water – just enough to form a firm dough. Shape into 12 small balls.
4 Add the dumplings to the goulash, cover and cook over a gentle heat for a further 20 minutes until the vegetables are tender and the dumplings light and fluffy.

Serves 4
Preparation time: 25 minutes
Cooking time: 55–60 minutes

Spicy Bean Burgers and Mango Salsa

The wonderful thing about these small, meatless burgers is the difference in
texture between the crispy outer crust and the light, creamy middle. The spice of
the chilli is balanced by the refreshing quality of the mango salsa.

- 1 tablespoon sunflower oil
- ½ large red onion, chopped finely
- 1 garlic clove, crushed
- 1 teaspoon grated fresh root ginger
- 1 teaspoon ground cumin
- 1 teaspoon ground coriander
- 2 teaspoons chilli powder
- 1 x 425 g/14 oz can red kidney beans, drained
- 75 g/3 oz fresh wholemeal breadcrumbs
- 2 tablespoons chopped fresh coriander
- 2 tablespoons dark soy sauce
- salt and pepper
- wholemeal flour, to dust
- vegetable oil, for shallow frying
- 4 sprigs of coriander, to garnish

MANGO SALSA:
- ½ small ripe mango
- 1 ripe tomato, skinned, deseeded and diced
- 1 red chilli, deseeded and chopped finely
- 1 tablespoon chopped fresh coriander
- 1 tablespoon chopped red onion
- 1 tablespoon lime juice
- pinch of sugar
- 1 tablespoon olive oil

1 Heat the oil in a frying pan, add the onion, garlic, ginger and spices and fry for
10 minutes. Remove from the heat and leave to cool slightly.
2 Put the onion mixture into a food processor with the beans, breadcrumbs,
coriander and soy sauce and blend until smooth; season to taste.
3 Make the salsa. Peel and stone the mango, finely chop the flesh and stir in all the
remaining ingredients. Cover and set aside for the flavours to develop.
4 With wet hands, form the bean mixture into 8 small burgers and coat lightly in
flour. Heat 1 cm/½ inch oil in a frying pan and fry the burgers in batches for 2–3
minutes on each side until crisp and golden. Drain on paper towels and keep warm
while cooking the rest. Serve at once with a spoonful of salsa, garnished with sprigs
of fresh coriander.

Serves 4
Preparation time: 45 minutes
Cooking time: 15 minutes

VARIATION
Substitute other drained beans such as borlotti or aduki beans for the kidney beans
and serve the burgers with a Fresh Tomato Sauce (see page 94).

Crusted Cassoulet

Cassoulet is a classic dish from southwest France, made with beans and sausages, duck, goose or other meats. This vegetarian version has a topping of sliced bread with garlic, thyme and grated cheese. Serve the cassoulet with a crisp green salad.

- 125 g/4 oz dried haricot beans, soaked overnight
- 1.2 litres/2 pints water
- 15 g/½ oz dried ceps
- 150 ml/¼ pint boiling water
- 6 tablespoons extra virgin olive oil
- 2 garlic cloves, chopped
- 250 g/8 oz baby onions, halved
- 175 g/6 oz mixed mushrooms, sliced
- 1 tablespoon each chopped fresh thyme, rosemary and sage
- 2 carrots, diced
- 2 celery sticks, sliced

- 1 red pepper, deseeded and diced
- 150 ml/¼ pint red wine
- 4 tablespoons tomato purée
- 1 tablespoon dark soy sauce
- salt and pepper

CRUST:

- ½ small French stick, sliced thinly
- 2 tablespoons extra virgin olive oil
- 1 garlic clove, crushed
- 2 tablespoons chopped fresh thyme
- 25 g/1 oz vegetarian Parmesan cheese, grated

1 Drain the beans and place in a saucepan with the water. Bring to the boil and boil rapidly for about 10 minutes. Lower the heat, cover and simmer gently for 45 minutes. Drain the beans and reserve 300 ml/½ pint of the cooking liquid.

2 Soak the dried ceps in the boiling water for 20 minutes, then drain, reserving the liquid. Slice the ceps.

3 Heat half the oil in a frying pan and fry the garlic and onions for 5 minutes. Add the mushrooms and herbs, and stir-fry for a further 5 minutes until the mushrooms are golden. Remove from the pan with a slotted spoon and set aside.

4 Heat the remaining oil in the frying pan and fry the carrots, celery and pepper for 5 minutes; add the wine and boil rapidly for 3 minutes. Stir in the beans and their liquid, the mushroom mixture, ceps and their liquid, tomato purée and soy sauce, season to taste. Spoon into 4 small dishes or 1 large gratin dish.

5 Layer the sliced bread over the casserole. Mix together the oil, garlic and thyme, brush over the bread and scatter with the Parmesan. Cover loosely with foil and place in a preheated oven, 190°C (375°F), Gas Mark 5, for 30 minutes. Remove the foil and bake for a further 20 minutes until the crust is golden.

Serves 6

Preparation time: 40 minutes, plus overnight soaking
Cooking time: 1½–1¾ hours
Oven temperature: 190°C (375°F), Gas Mark 5

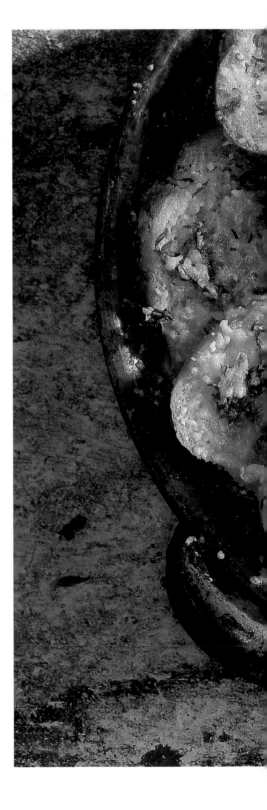

Pizzas and Bread

Soda Bread with Oatmeal

375 g/12 oz plain wholemeal flour, plus extra for dusting
50 g/2 oz pinhead oatmeal
1 teaspoon bicarbonate of soda
½ teaspoon salt
300 ml/½ pint buttermilk or natural yogurt

1 In a bowl mix together the flour, oatmeal, bicarbonate of soda and salt. Make a well in the centre and gradually work in the buttermilk or yogurt to form a soft dough.
2 Turn out on to a lightly floured surface and knead gently for 5 minutes until the dough is smooth.
3 Shape the dough into a flattish round and place on a greased baking sheet. Using a sharp knife, slash a cross on the top of the bread and place in a preheated oven, 230°C (450°F), Gas Mark 8, for 15 minutes. Reduce the temperature to 200°C (400°F), Gas Mark 6 and continue to bake for a further 30 minutes until the bread is risen and golden and sounds hollow when tapped on the bottom.
4 Wrap the bread in a clean tea towel and leave to cool completely on a wire rack. Slice and serve with butter and jam or marmalade.

Makes 1 small loaf
Preparation time: 5 minutes
Cooking time: 50 minutes
Oven temperature: 230°C (450°F), Gas Mark 8, then 200°C (400°F), Gas Mark 6

leave to rise in a warm, draught-free place for about 45 minutes or until doubled in size.

4 Knock back the dough by gently kneading it once more, and shape into an oval loaf. Place the loaf on an oiled baking sheet, cover with oiled polythene and leave to rise for a further 20 minutes. Brush the surface of the loaf with water and scatter over extra oats.

5 Slash the top several times and place in a preheated oven, 220°C (425°F), Gas Mark 7, for 35–40 minutes until the bread is risen and sounds hollow when tapped on the bottom. Leave to cool completely on a wire rack before slicing.

Makes 1 large loaf
Preparation time: 10 minutes, plus about 1 hour rising
Cooking time: 40 minutes
Oven temperature: 220°C (425°F), Gas Mark 7

VARIATION

Hazelnut and Apricot Bread

For a different flavour substitute an equal amount of hazelnuts and chopped ready-to-eat dried apricots for the walnuts and sultanas.

Walnut and Sultana Bread

- 15 g/½ oz fresh yeast
- 500 g/1 lb granary flour, plus extra for dusting
- 1 teaspoon sugar
- 300 ml/½ pint warm water
- 1 teaspoon salt
- 25 g/1 oz butter
- 50 g/2 oz organic oats, plus extra for sprinkling
- 50 g/2 oz walnuts, chopped roughly
- 50 g/2 oz sultanas
- 2 tablespoons malt extract
- vegetable oil, for oiling

1 Blend the yeast with 4 tablespoons of the flour, the sugar and half the water until well combined and leave in a warm place for 10 minutes until it is frothy.

2 In a large bowl mix together the remaining flour and salt, rub in the butter and stir in the oats, nuts and sultanas. Make a well in the centre and gradually work in the frothed yeast, malt extract and remaining water to form a stiff dough.

3 Turn out on to a lightly floured surface and knead for 8–10 minutes until the dough is smooth and elastic. Place in an oiled bowl, turn once to coat the dough with oil, cover and

Basic Pizza Dough with Rosemary, Garlic and Olive Oil

- 250 g/8 oz strong plain flour, plus extra for dusting
- ½ teaspoon salt
- ½ teaspoon fast-action dried yeast
- 125 ml/4 fl oz warm water
- 1 tablespoon extra virgin olive oil, plus extra for oiling

TOPPING:

- 6 tablespoons extra virgin olive oil
- 3 garlic cloves, crushed
- 3 tablespoons chopped fresh rosemary
- sea salt and pepper

1 Sift the flour and salt into a large bowl and stir in the dried yeast. Make a well in the centre and gradually stir in the water and oil to form a soft dough.

2 Turn out on to a lightly floured surface and knead for 8–10 minutes until smooth and elastic. Place in an oiled bowl, turn once to coat the dough with oil and cover with oiled clingfilm. Leave to rise in a warm, draught-free place for 45 minutes or until doubled in size.

3 Meanwhile, prepare the topping: mix together the oil, garlic and rosemary and leave to stand.

4 Lightly knead the risen dough, divide in half and roll out each piece to a 23 cm/9 inch round. Transfer the rounds to 2 oiled pizza plates or a large oiled baking sheet. Prick with a fork and carefully spread with the rosemary oil. Sprinkle over plenty of sea salt and pepper.

5 Place at the top of a preheated oven, 220°C (425°F), Gas Mark 7, for 15 minutes until lightly risen, crisp and golden. Serve at once.

Makes 2 x 23 cm/9 inch pizzas
Preparation time: 15 minutes, plus 45 minutes rising
Cooking time: 15 minutes
Oven temperature: 220°C (425°F), Gas Mark 7

Many Tomato Pizza

- 1 quantity Basic Pizza Dough (see page 51)
- extra virgin olive oil, for oiling and drizzling

TOPPING:

- 2 large ripe plum tomatoes, sliced
- 125 g/4 oz red cherry tomatoes, halved
- 125 g/4 oz yellow pear tomatoes, halved
- 4 sun-dried tomatoes in oil, drained and chopped roughly
- handful of basil leaves, torn into pieces
- 2 teaspoons grated lemon rind
- 12 black olives, pitted
- sea salt and pepper

1 Make up the dough according to the recipe on page 51 and leave to rise once.
2 Lightly knead the risen dough, divide in half and roll out each piece to a 23 cm/ 9 inch round. Transfer to 2 oiled pizza plates or a large oiled baking sheet.
3 Dry the tomato slices on paper towels. Arrange all the tomatoes over the pizzas, scattering over the basil, lemon rind and black olives. Season well and drizzle over a little extra olive oil.
4 Place at the top of a preheated oven, 230°C (450°F), Gas Mark 8, for 20 minutes until the bases are crisp and the tops golden. Serve at once.

Serves 2

Preparation time: 10 minutes, plus making dough and rising
Cooking time: 20 minutes
Oven temperature: 230°C (450°F), Gas Mark 8

VARIATION

Pizza Margherita

- 1 quantity Basic Pizza Dough (see page 51)
- extra virgin olive oil, for oiling and drizzling

TOPPING:

- ½ quantity Quick Tomato Sauce (see page 94)
- 300 g/10 oz mozzarella cheese, drained, dried and diced
- 12 black olives, pitted (optional)

1 Make up the dough according to the recipe on page 51 and leave to rise once.
2 Lightly knead the risen dough, divide in half and roll out each piece to a 25 cm/10 inch round. Transfer to 2 oiled pizza plates or a large oiled baking sheet.
3 Divide the tomato sauce between the 2 pizza bases and spread to within 5 mm/¼ inch of the edge. Sprinkle over the cheese and olives and drizzle over a little oil.
4 Place at the top of a preheated oven, 230°C (450°F), Gas Mark 8, for 20 minutes until the bases are crisp, the tops golden and the cheese bubbling.

Serves 2

Preparation time: 10 minutes, plus making dough and rising
Cooking time: 20 minutes
Oven temperature: 230°C (450°F), Gas Mark 8

Vegetable Calzone

A calzone is a stuffed pizza (or one that is simply folded in half and sealed). There are as many fillings for calzone as toppings for pizza. Spinach and mozzarella is a good combination; you could add sun-dried tomatoes or fresh herbs.

- **double quantity Basic Pizza Dough (see page 51)**
- **extra virgin olive oil**

FILLING:

- **1 tablespoon extra virgin olive oil**
- **1 large onion, sliced thinly**
- **1 red pepper, cored, deseeded and sliced**
- **1 garlic clove, crushed**
- **500 g/1 lb frozen leaf spinach, thawed**
- **175 g/6 oz mozzarella cheese, diced**
- **50 g/2 oz pine nuts, toasted**
- **40 g/1½ oz sultanas**
- **¼ teaspoon grated nutmeg**
- **salt and pepper**

1 Make up a double quantity of pizza dough according to the recipe on page 51 and leave to rise once.
2 Meanwhile, prepare the filling. Heat the oil in a frying pan, add the onion, pepper and garlic and fry for 5 minutes until golden. Drain the spinach, squeeze out any excess liquid and chop finely. Stir into the onion mixture and remove from the heat. Stir in all the remaining ingredients and set aside to cool.
3 Lightly knead the risen dough and divide into 6 equal pieces. Roll out each piece to an 18 cm/7 inch round. Divide the filling between the rounds, brush the edges with water and fold the dough over, pressing together firmly to seal the edges and enclose the filling.
4 Transfer the parcels to a large oiled baking sheet and lightly brush each one with water. Place at the top of a preheated oven, 200°C (400°F), Gas Mark 6, for 20 minutes until the calzone are golden. Remove from the oven and leave to rest for 10 minutes before serving.

Serves 6
Preparation time: 30 minutes, plus making dough and rising
Cooking time: 25–30 minutes
Oven temperature: 200°C (400°F), Gas Mark 6

Californian Pizza

This is similar to the southern French classic Pissaladière, which is a tomato-less pizza, topped with onions, anchovies and capers and occasionally a few black olives.

- 1 quantity Basic Pizza Dough (see page 51)
- 2 tablespoons extra virgin olive oil, plus extra for oiling
- 1 kg/2 lb red onions, sliced thinly
- 2 tablespoons chopped fresh thyme
- ½ teaspoon salt
- ½ teaspoon sugar
- 175 g/6 oz dolcelatte cheese, crumbled
- 50 g/2 oz pitted black olives
- sea salt and pepper

1 Make up the dough according to the recipe on page 51 and leave to rise once.

2 Meanwhile, heat the oil in a large heavy-bottomed frying pan, add the onions, thyme, salt and sugar and cook over a medium heat for 25 minutes until golden and caramelized. Drain off any juices and set aside. Place a large baking sheet at the top of a preheated oven, 220°C (425°F), Gas Mark 7.

3 Lightly knead the risen dough and roll out on a lightly floured surface to form a 23 x 33 cm/9 x 13 inch rectangle. Press into an oiled Swiss roll tin the same size as the dough. Brush the surface with a little oil, spread over the onion mixture and scatter with the cheese and olives. Season to taste.

4 Place the tin on the hot baking sheet in the oven and bake for 20 minutes until golden. Serve hot or leave to cool to room temperature.

Serves 4–6
Preparation time: 25 minutes, plus making dough and rising
Cooking time: 45 minutes
Oven temperature: 220°C (425°F), Gas Mark 7

Pastries and Pies

Spinach and Chick Pea Flan

1 quantity Shortcrust Pastry (see page 58)

175 g/6 oz fresh spinach leaves

2 tablespoons extra virgin olive oil

1 small onion, sliced thinly

2 garlic cloves, crushed

1 teaspoon ground turmeric

200 g/7 oz canned chick peas, drained

2 eggs, lightly beaten

200 ml/7 fl oz single cream

pinch of grated nutmeg

salt and pepper

1 On a lightly floured surface, roll out the pastry and use to line a deep, 20 cm/8 inch flan tin. Prick the base; chill for a further 20 minutes. Line with foil and baking beans; place in a preheated oven, 200°C (400°F), Gas Mark 6, for 10 minutes. Remove the foil and beans and bake for a further 10–12 minutes until the pastry is crisp.
2 Wash the spinach and place in a large saucepan. Heat gently for 3–4 minutes until the spinach wilts. Drain, squeeze out all the excess liquid and chop finely.
3 Heat the oil in a saucepan, add the onion, garlic and turmeric, fry for 5 minutes. Stir in the chick peas and spinach; remove from the heat. Spread over the pastry case.
4 Beat the eggs, cream, nutmeg and seasoning together and pour into the pastry case. Bake for 35–40 minutes until firm and golden.

Serves 6–8
Preparation time: 15 minutes, plus making pastry and chilling
Cooking time: 1 hour–1 hour 10 minutes
Oven temperature: 200°C (400°F), Gas Mark 6

Courgette, Sun-dried Tomato and Ricotta Flan

If ricotta cheese is not available, curd cheese can be substituted.

- 1 quantity Shortcrust Pastry (see right)
- 2 tablespoons extra virgin olive oil
- 1 small onion, sliced thinly
- 2 courgettes, sliced thinly
- 50 g/2 oz drained sun-dried tomatoes in oil, sliced
- 250 g/8 oz ricotta or curd cheese
- 2 tablespoons milk
- 2 eggs, beaten
- 4 tablespoons chopped fresh herbs (basil, rosemary, sage, thyme)
- 12 black olives, pitted and halved
- salt and pepper

1 On a lightly floured surface, roll out the pastry and use to line a 23 cm/9 inch flan tin. Prick the base and chill for a further 20 minutes. Line the pastry case with foil and baking beans and place in a preheated oven, 200°C (400°F), Gas Mark 6, for 10 minutes. Remove the foil and beans and bake for a further 10–12 minutes until the pastry is crisp and golden.
2 Heat the oil in a frying pan, add the onion and courgettes and fry gently for 5–6 minutes until lightly golden. Scatter over the base of the pastry case and top with the sun-dried tomatoes.

3 Beat the ricotta, milk, eggs, herbs and salt and pepper together and spread over the courgette mixture. Scatter over the olives and bake for 30–35 minutes until firm and golden.

Serves 6–8
Preparation time: 20 minutes, plus making pastry and chilling
Cooking time: 55–60 minutes
Oven temperature: 200°C (400°F), Gas Mark 6

Shortcrust Pastry

- 175 g/6 oz plain flour, plus extra for dusting
- ½ teaspoon salt
- 75 g/3 oz butter, diced
- 2–3 tablespoons cold water

1 Sift the flour and salt into a bowl and rub in the butter until the mixture resembles fine breadcrumbs. Gradually work in enough water to form a soft dough.
2 On a lightly floured surface, knead the dough until smooth, then wrap in clingfilm and chill for 30 minutes before using.

Makes 300 g/10 oz pastry, enough to line a 23–25 cm/ 9–10 inch flan tin
Preparation time: 5–10 minutes, plus chilling

Asparagus, Walnut and Parmesan Quiche

The egg custard is enriched with a garlic purée, adding a wonderfully mellow flavour without overpowering the asparagus.

- 1 quantity Shortcrust Pastry (see left)
- 10 whole garlic cloves, peeled
- 2 tablespoons extra virgin olive oil
- 375 g/12 oz asparagus spears
- 40 g/1½ oz walnuts, toasted and chopped
- 200 ml/7 fl oz single cream or milk
- 3 eggs, lightly beaten
- 75 g/3 oz vegetarian Parmesan cheese, grated
- salt and pepper

1 On a lightly floured surface, roll out the pastry and use to line a deep, 23 cm/9 inch flan tin. Prick the base with a fork and chill for a further 20 minutes.

2 Meanwhile, cook the garlic cloves in boiling water for 10 minutes, drain and pat dry. Mash with 1 tablespoon of the oil to form a paste.

3 Line the pastry case with foil and baking beans and place in a preheated oven, 200°C (400°F), Gas Mark 6, for 10 minutes. Remove the foil and beans from the pastry case and bake for a further 10–12 minutes until the pastry is crisp and golden. Reduce the oven temperature to 190°C (375°F), Gas Mark 5.

4 Heat the remaining oil and stir-fry the asparagus spears for 5 minutes. Scatter the asparagus spears over the pastry case together with the walnuts. Beat together the cream or milk, garlic paste, eggs, Parmesan and salt and pepper, pour over the asparagus and bake for 25 minutes until set and golden brown.

Serves 6–8
Preparation time: 15 minutes, plus making pastry and chilling
Cooking time: 50 minutes
Oven temperature: 200°C (400°F), Gas Mark 6, then 190°C (375°F), Gas Mark 5

Aubergine and Pasta Timbale

In this Italian dish, cooked pasta is mixed with a sauce and baked in a cake tin or mould. Here the tin is lined with grilled aubergine slices.

- 4 tablespoons extra virgin olive oil
- 50 g/2 oz Parmesan cheese, grated
- 4 long thin aubergines, about 250 g/8 oz each, trimmed
- 250 g/8 oz dried penne pasta
- ½ quantity Quick Tomato Sauce (see page 94)
- 150 ml/¼ pint double cream
- salt and pepper

1 Brush a 20 cm/8 inch cake tin with oil and sprinkle liberally with some of

the Parmesan. Set to one side.
2 Cut a thin slice from one side of each aubergine and discard, then repeat on the opposite side. Cut the aubergines lengthways into 5 thin slices. Brush each slice with a little olive oil and place under a preheated hot grill. Cook for 4–5 minutes on each side until charred and softened.
3 Leave the aubergine slices to cool slightly, then use to line the base and sides of the tin, overlapping the slices slightly and letting the ends protrude over the edge of the tin. Of the remaining aubergine slices, reserve two and finely chop the rest.
4 Cook the pasta according to the packet instructions until al dente, drain well and transfer to a bowl. Stir in the tomato sauce, cream, chopped aubergines if any and the remaining Parmesan cheese, season well.
5 Spoon into the tin, place the two aubergine slices in the centre and fold over the protruding ends to enclose the filling. Cover loosely with foil and place in a preheated oven, 190°C (375°F), Gas Mark 5, for 40 minutes until the centre feels firm to the touch.
6 Remove from the oven and leave to stand for 15 minutes. Turn out and serve cut into wedges, with a green salad and Italian bread.

Serves 6–8
Preparation time: 30 minutes
Cooking time: 1 hour, plus
15 minutes resting
Oven temperature: 190°C (375°F),
Gas Mark 5

VARIATION

Gratin of Aubergine, Mushrooms and Pasta

- 4 tablespoons extra virgin olive oil
- 1 onion, chopped
- 2 garlic cloves, crushed
- 250 g/8 oz button mushrooms
- 1 aubergine, chopped roughly
- 375 g/12 oz cooked conchiglie pasta
- 600 ml/1 pint double cream
- 50 g/2 oz Parmesan cheese, grated
- salt and pepper

1 Heat the oil in a frying pan and fry the onion and garlic for 5 minutes. Add the mushrooms, stir-fry for 5 minutes, then, using a slotted spoon, transfer to a large bowl.
2 Fry the chopped aubergine in the remaining oil for 5–6 minutes until golden. Add to the mushrooms and stir in the cooked pasta; season to taste. Spoon into a oiled gratin dish, pour over the cream and sprinkle all over with the cheese. Place the gratin in a preheated oven, 190°C (375°F), Gas Mark 5, for about 30 minutes until bubbling and golden.

Serves 6
Preparation time: 10 minutes
Cooking time: 45 minutes
Oven temperature: 190°C (375°F),
Gas Mark 5

Rich Vegetable Pie in Flaky Pastry

This rich savoury pie will give comfort on a cold day.

- 4 tablespoons extra virgin olive oil
- 500 g/1 lb button mushrooms, halved
- 2 garlic cloves, crushed
- 250 g/8 oz baby onions, halved
- 250 g/8 oz parsnips, chopped
- 250 g/8 oz carrots, chopped
- 2 tablespoons chopped fresh thyme
- 1 tablespoon chopped fresh sage
- 300 ml/½ pint full-bodied dry red wine
- 1 x 425 g/14 oz can chopped tomatoes
- 150 ml/¼ pint Vegetable Stock (see page 94)
- 2 tablespoons tomato purée
- 2 tablespoons dark soy sauce
- 1 quantity Flaky Pastry (see right)
- Egg Glaze (see page 9)
- salt and pepper

1 Heat half the oil in a frying pan, add the mushrooms and garlic and stir-fry for 3–4 minutes until golden. Remove from the pan and set aside.
2 Add the remaining oil to the pan and fry the onions, parsnips, carrots and herbs for 10 minutes. Add the wine and boil rapidly for 3 minutes. Stir in the tomatoes, stock, tomato purée and soy sauce. Bring to the boil, cover and simmer for 30 minutes.
3 Add the mushrooms, season to taste, transfer to a 1.75 litre/3 pint pie dish and set aside.
4 On a lightly floured surface, roll out the pastry to a little larger than the pie dish. Cut 4 strips, 2.5 cm/ 1 inch wide, from around the edge of the pastry and press on to the rim of the dish, wetting the rim as you go.
5 Lay the remaining pastry over the pie, trim the edges and press together, wetting the pastry to seal. Flute the edges and use any trimmings to make shapes to decorate the pie.
6 Brush the pastry with egg glaze and bake in a preheated oven, 220°C (425°F), Gas Mark 7, for 20 minutes, then reduce the temperature to 200°C (400°F), Gas Mark 6, and bake for a further 15 minutes.

Serves 6
Preparation time: 30 minutes, plus making pastry and chilling
Cooking time: 1 hour 20 minutes
Oven temperature: 220°C (425°F), Gas Mark 7, then 200°C (400°F), Gas Mark 6

Flaky Pastry

This recipe is illustrated in the step-by-step photographs on page 9.

- 200 g/7 oz plain flour
- 1 teaspoon salt
- 125 g/4 oz butter or hard vegetable margarine
- 100 ml/3½ fl oz cold water

1 Sift the flour and salt into a bowl and rub in 25 g/1 oz of the butter or margarine. Gradually work in the water to form a soft dough. Turn out on to a lightly floured surface and knead gently until smooth.
2 Roll out the dough to an oblong about 5 mm/¼ inch thick. Dot 25 g/1 oz of the remaining butter or margarine over two-thirds of the surface of the dough, folding the uncovered third back over half the covered dough and finally folding the remaining dough back over that, enclosing all the butter.
3 Seal the edges by pressing firmly with the rolling pin. Turn the dough once to the left and roll out to an oblong again. Repeat the process, then wrap and chill for 10 minutes.
4 Repeat the dotting and folding one final time and then re-roll a further 2 times without butter. Wrap and chill the dough for at least 30 minutes before using.

Makes 425 g/14 oz pastry
Preparation time: 20 minutes, plus chilling time

Filo Pie with Seaweed Filling

There are several varieties of edible seaweed; most are rich sources of useful minerals. Dulse seaweed is sold dried and is similar to Japanese nori, which could be used instead.

- 4 tablespoons extra virgin olive oil, plus extra for brushing
- 1 onion, chopped finely
- 1 garlic clove, crushed
- 2 teaspoons grated fresh root ginger
- 175 g/6 oz button mushrooms
- 50 g/2 oz dried dulse seaweed
- 1 tablespoon dark soy sauce
- 1 tablespoon lemon juice
- 2 tablespoons chopped fresh coriander
- 50 g/2 oz fresh white breadcrumbs
- 50 g/2 oz pine nuts
- 2 tablespoons sesame seeds
- 12 sheets filo pastry, thawed if frozen
- pepper
- Onion and Wine Gravy (see page 95), to serve

1 Heat half the oil in a large frying pan, add the onion, garlic and ginger and fry gently for 5 minutes. Add the mushrooms and fry for a further 5 minutes, stirring frequently.

2 Using a pair of scissors, cut the seaweed into small pieces. Add to the pan with the soy sauce, lemon juice and coriander. Stir over a low heat until the seaweed is softened, then remove from the heat.

3 In another pan, heat the remaining oil and stir-fry the breadcrumbs, pine nuts and sesame seeds for 4–5 minutes until evenly browned. Remove from the heat.

4 Keeping the filo pastry covered with a clean tea towel, take one sheet at a time and trim to fit into an oiled 20 x 30 cm/8 x 12 inch roasting tin. Press into the base and brush with oil. Scatter on 2 teaspoons of the breadcrumb mixture.

5 Repeat with 5 more sheets of pastry, and half the breadcrumb mixture. Spread over the seaweed mixture and then repeat the layers of pastry and breadcrumbs, ending with a layer of pastry.

6 Brush liberally with oil, mark into 6 portions with a sharp knife and place in a preheated oven, 190°C (375°F), Gas Mark 5, for 30 minutes until crisp and golden, covering with foil if the top becomes too brown. Serve hot with the onion and wine gravy and a selection of steamed vegetables.

Serves 6
Preparation time: 25 minutes, plus making gravy and steaming vegetables
Cooking time: 45 minutes
Oven temperature: 190°C (375°F), Gas Mark 5

Mediterranean Suet Parcel

The texture of this suet pastry is particularly good: crisp on the outside with a light fluffy centre. The grilled vegetables for the filling can be prepared in advance.

- 500 g/1 lb self-raising flour
- 1 teaspoon salt
- 175 g/6 oz vegetable suet
- 150 ml/¼ pint natural yogurt
- 200 ml/7 fl oz milk

FILLING:

- 2 aubergines
- 2 tablespoons extra virgin olive oil
- 2 large red peppers, cored, deseeded and quartered
- 4 firm ripe tomatoes, sliced
- 12 large basil leaves
- 175 g/6 oz mozzarella cheese, sliced thinly
- Egg Glaze (see page 9)
- Mushroom Gravy (see page 95), to serve

1 Sift the flour and salt into a large bowl, stir in the suet and then gradually work in the yogurt and milk to form a stiff dough. Knead lightly until smooth, wrap and leave to rest while preparing the filling.
2 Cut the aubergines lengthways into thick slices, brush with a little oil and place under a preheated hot grill for 5–6 minutes on each side until golden and tender. Grill the pepper quarters for 6–8 minutes until charred and tender, wrap in a plastic bag and leave until cool enough to handle. Peel off the skin.
3 On a lightly floured surface, roll out the dough to a 35 cm/14 inch square. Arrange the aubergines, peppers, tomatoes, basil and cheese in layers, diagonally in the centre of the pastry, forming a 20 cm/8 inch square shape.
4 Dampen the edges of the pastry with a little water and draw up the 4 corners, pressing together in the middle to seal in the filling.
5 Transfer the parcel to a baking sheet, brush with egg glaze and place in a preheated oven, 200°C (400°F), Gas Mark 6, for 30 minutes. Reduce the temperature to 180°C (350°F), Gas Mark 4, and bake for a further 15 minutes until puffed up and golden. Leave to rest for 5 minutes, then serve hot, with mushroom gravy and a green salad.

Serves 6
Preparation time: 40 minutes, plus making gravy
Cooking time: 1 hour
Oven temperature: 200°C (400°F), Gas Mark 6, then 180°C (350°F), Gas Mark 4

Vegetables and Salads

Tomato and Coriander Salad

1 kg/2 lb mixed tomatoes, sliced or quartered – use yellow cherry tomatoes if available

2 teaspoons grated lime rind

½ small red onion, sliced thinly

1 tablespoon sesame seeds, toasted (optional)

DRESSING:

2 tablespoons chopped fresh coriander

1 tablespoon lime juice

1 garlic clove, crushed

½ teaspoon clear honey

pinch of cayenne pepper

4 tablespoons extra virgin olive oil

salt and pepper

1 First make the dressing. Whisk together the coriander, lime juice, garlic, honey, cayenne and salt and pepper and then whisk in the oil.

2 Arrange the tomatoes in a large serving bowl and scatter over the lime rind, onion and toasted sesame seeds, if using.

3 Whisk the dressing ingredients once more and pour over the salad. Cover the salad and set aside for 30 minutes for the flavours to develop before serving.

Serves 4

Preparation time: 5 minutes, plus 30 minutes marinating

Mesclun with Croûtons and Cheese Dressing

Mesclun is a French salad using a mixture of wild salad leaves and herbs. Its clean, fresh taste is emphasized with this tangy cheese dressing: it makes the perfect first course on a hot summer day.

- 250 g/8 oz mixed salad leaves
- 25 g/1 oz flat leaf parsley
- 4 thick slices of day-old white bread
- 1 large garlic clove, halved

DRESSING:
- 25 g/1 oz dolcelatte cheese, softened
- 25 g/1 oz ricotta cheese, softened
- 6 tablespoons extra virgin olive oil
- 1 tablespoon white wine vinegar
- 1 tablespoon boiling water
- salt and pepper

1 Wash all the salad leaves and the parsley, shake off the excess water and transfer to a plastic bag. Tie the bag and chill for 30 minutes.
2 To make the dressing, place both the cheeses in a bowl and gradually beat in the oil, vinegar, boiling water and salt and pepper to form a smooth, thick sauce.

3 Place the salad leaves in a large bowl. Toast the bread lightly on both sides and, while still warm, rub all over with the garlic. Cut the bread into cubes and add to the bowl with the salad leaves.
4 Pour the dressing over the salad leaves, toss well and serve at once.

Serves 4
Preparation time: 10 minutes, plus 30 minutes chilling
Cooking time: 2–3 minutes

Country Salad with Horseradish Dressing

A cornucopia of garden vegetables combine to make a satisfying and robust salad. When hard-boiling the eggs, carefully spoon them into a pan of gently simmering water. Return to the boil and cook for 8 minutes. Drain and plunge into cold water. Peel and halve when required.

- 250 g/8 oz shelled broad beans
- 125 g/4 oz green beans, halved
- 500 g/1 lb firm ripe plum tomatoes, cut into wedges
- ½ small cucumber, sliced thickly
- 2 celery sticks, sliced
- 175 g/6 oz cooked beetroot, sliced
- 1 small red onion, sliced thinly
- 2 tablespoons drained capers
- 2 soft, hard-boiled eggs (see above), peeled and halved
- salt

DRESSING:

- 2 tablespoons grated horseradish or 1 tablespoon creamed horseradish
- 4 tablespoons extra virgin olive oil
- 2 teaspoons red wine vinegar
- pinch of sugar
- 2 tablespoons chopped fresh herbs

1 Blanch the broad beans in boiling, salted water for 1 minute, drain, refresh under cold water and pat dry on paper towels. Peel and discard the tough outer skin. Blanch the green beans for 1 minute, drain, refresh under cold water and pat dry on paper towels.

2 Place the beans in a large bowl and add the tomatoes, cucumber, celery, beetroot, onion and capers.

3 Whisk all the dressing ingredients together and season to taste. Pour over the salad and toss gently until all the ingredients are evenly coated with the dressing. Transfer the salad to a serving dish and top with the egg halves. Serve at once.

Serves 4

Preparation time: 20 minutes
Cooking time: 10 minutes

Charred Leek Salad with Hazelnuts

- 500 g/1 lb baby leeks
- 1–2 tablespoons hazelnut oil
- dash of lemon juice
- 40 g/1½ oz blanched hazelnuts
- 2 little gem or Cos lettuce hearts
- a few mint sprigs
- 15 g/½ oz pecorino cheese
- 20 black olives, to garnish

DRESSING:

- 4 tablespoons hazelnut oil
- 2 tablespoons extra virgin olive oil
- 2 teaspoons sherry vinegar
- salt and pepper

1 Brush the leeks with a little hazelnut oil and griddle or grill, turning frequently, for 6–8 minutes, until evenly browned and cooked through. Toss with a dash of lemon juice and season to taste with salt and pepper. Set aside to cool.

2 Meanwhile, dry-fry the nuts until browned, cool and then chop roughly. Separate the lettuce leaves and pull the mint leaves from the stalks.

3 Arrange the leeks in bowls or on plates and top with the lettuce leaves, mint and nuts. Whisk together the dressing ingredients and pour over the salad. Shave the pecorino over the salad and serve garnished with the olives.

Serves 4
Preparation time: 10 minutes
Cooking time: 15 minutes

Warm Salad of Griddled Beetroot and Parsnips

Beetroot and parsnips go together surprisingly well, as well as making an attractive visual contrast.

- 500 g/1 lb raw beetroot, peeled and cut into 1 cm/½ inch thick slices
- 500 g/1 lb parsnips, peeled and cut into 1 cm/½ inch thick slices
- 4 tablespoons soured cream
- 3 tablespoons water
- 1 bunch of dill, chopped
- sea salt and pepper

1 Heat a griddle pan. Griddle the beetroot slices on each side for 4–5 minutes. Remove and keep warm. Repeat until all the slices are cooked.
2 Griddle the parsnip slices on each side for 4–5 minutes, remove and add to the beetroot. Repeat until all the slices are cooked.
3 Mix together the soured cream, water, dill and salt and pepper to taste. Drizzle the dressing over the beetroot and parsnips and serve.

Serves 4
Preparation time: 10 minutes
Cooking time: 20 minutes

Roasted Vegetable and Bread Salad

- 1 large aubergine, cubed
- 4 courgettes, cubed
- 2 red peppers, cored, deseeded and sliced
- 4 whole garlic cloves, peeled
- extra virgin olive oil
- 4 firm ripe tomatoes, diced
- 175 g/6 oz day-old bread, diced
- 4 tablespoons chopped fresh basil

DRESSING:
- 9 tablespoons extra virgin olive oil
- 2 tablespoons red wine vinegar
- pinch of sugar
- 3 tablespoons boiling water
- salt and pepper

1 Toss the aubergine, courgettes, peppers and garlic cloves with about 4 tablespoons of olive oil and place in a large roasting pan. Bake in a preheated oven, 220°C (425°F), Gas Mark 7, for 50 minutes.

2 Remove the pan from the oven and stir in the tomatoes, with a little extra oil if necessary. Whisk the dressing ingredients together, except the water, and season to taste. Stir 3 tablespoons of the dressing into the vegetables and leave to cool.

3 Place the bread in a bowl. Add the boiling water to the remaining dressing and stir to mix with the bread; leave to soak for 10 minutes.

4 Just before serving, add the bread to the roasted vegetables together with the basil and then season to taste. Transfer the salad to a large serving dish and then serve at room temperature.

Serves 4
Preparation time: 25 minutes, plus cooling
Cooking time: 50 minutes
Oven temperature: 220°C (425°F), Gas Mark 7

Lemon Rice and Wild Rice Salad with Nuts, Seeds and Papaya

This truly unusual mixed rice salad combines a delicious tangy flavour with an interesting crunchy texture.

- 50 g/2 oz wild rice, rinsed
- 250 g/8 oz long-grain rice, rinsed
- 2 tablespoons lemon juice
- 1 teaspoon sugar
- 1 teaspoon salt
- 1 small papaya
- 1 bunch of spring onions, sliced
- 25 g/1 oz pecan nuts, toasted and chopped
- 25 g/1 oz brazil nuts, toasted and chopped
- 25 g/1 oz sunflower seeds, toasted
- 1 tablespoon poppy seeds

DRESSING:
- 6 tablespoons extra virgin olive oil
- 1 tablespoon lemon juice or lime juice
- 2 tablespoons chopped fresh parsley
- salt and pepper

1 Cook the wild rice in plenty of lightly salted, boiling water for 35 minutes until tender.

2 Meanwhile, put the long-grain rice in a pan with plenty of cold water, add the lemon juice, sugar and salt, bring to the boil and simmer gently for 10–12 minutes until cooked.

3 Drain both the wild and long-grain rice and place in a large bowl. Blend all the dressing ingredients together, season and toss with the rice. Set aside until cold.

4 Just before serving, cut the papaya in half, discard the seeds, peel and dice the flesh. Add to the rice with the spring onions, nuts and seeds. Taste and adjust the seasoning, if necessary, and serve at once.

Serves 6
Preparation time: 15 minutes
Cooking time: 35 minutes

Spiced Okra

Okra combines perfectly with the flavour of tomatoes and the warmth of Indian spices to provide a delicious vegetable accompaniment.

- 1 teaspoon cumin seeds
- 1 teaspoon coriander seeds
- 2 teaspoons mustard seeds
- 2 teaspoons sunflower oil
- 1 large onion, chopped
- 2 garlic cloves, crushed
- 2 teaspoons grated fresh root ginger
- 4 ripe tomatoes, chopped
- 1 teaspoon ground turmeric
- 1 teaspoon chilli powder
- 500 g/1 lb okra
- 150 ml/¼ pint Vegetable Stock (see page 94)
- 2 tablespoons chopped fresh coriander
- salt and pepper

1 Dry-fry the cumin, coriander and mustard seeds in a small frying pan until they start to pop and give off a smoky aroma. Remove from the heat and grind to form a rough powder.

2 Heat the oil in a saucepan, add the onion, garlic and ginger and fry over a medium heat for 10 minutes until golden. Stir in the tomatoes, cover and continue to cook for a further 10 minutes.

3 Add the roasted spices, turmeric and chilli powder, okra and stock. Bring to the boil, cover and simmer over a very low heat for 20 minutes until the okra is tender. Stir in the fresh coriander and season to taste. Serve hot.

Serves 4
Preparation time: 15 minutes
Cooking time: 40 minutes

Herbed Pasta Salad with Courgettes and Tomatoes

Toss the pasta with the herb dressing as soon as it is drained: this way the pasta will absorb the flavours.

- 250 g/8 oz dried pasta
- 250 g/8 oz baby courgettes, sliced very thinly
- 175 g/6 oz cherry tomatoes, halved
- 2 tablespoons pine nuts, toasted

DRESSING:

- 4 tablespoons extra virgin olive oil
- 1 tablespoon drained capers
- 1 tablespoon chopped fresh parsley
- 1 tablespoon chopped fresh basil
- 1 teaspoon grated lime rind
- 1 tablespoon white wine vinegar
- salt and pepper

TO GARNISH:

- coriander sprigs
- basil sprigs

1 Bring a large pan of water to a rolling boil, add the pasta, return to the boil and simmer for 10 minutes until the pasta is al dente.
2 Meanwhile, prepare the dressing. Place the ingredients in a liquidizer and process until fairly smooth. Taste and adjust the seasoning.
3 Drain the cooked pasta and immediately toss with the dressing. Stir in the courgettes and tomatoes and leave to cool to room temperature. Scatter over the pine nuts and serve garnished with fresh coriander and basil sprigs.

Serves 4
Preparation time: 15 minutes
Cooking time: 10 minutes

Grilled Asparagus with Walnut Sauce

Grilling asparagus gives this vegetable a really intense flavour. To serve as a starter, transfer the grilled asparagus to individual gratin dishes, spread over the sauce and return to the grill.

- 1 kg/2 lb asparagus spears, trimmed

WALNUT SAUCE:

- 50 g/2 oz walnuts, toasted
- 2 large spring onions, chopped very finely
- 1 garlic clove, crushed
- 1 teaspoon grated lemon rind
- 1 tablespoon chopped fresh basil
- 1 tablespoon chopped fresh parsley
- 4 tablespoons walnut oil, plus extra for brushing
- 50 ml/2 fl oz milk
- 25 g/1 oz vegetarian Parmesan cheese, grated (optional)

1 First make the sauce. Grind the walnuts with the spring onions, garlic, lemon rind and herbs. Whisk in the oil and then the milk to form a smooth sauce of a fairly thick pouring consistency.

2 Brush the asparagus spears with oil and place under a preheated hot grill for 5–6 minutes, turning frequently until golden and tender.

3 Transfer the grilled asparagus to a warmed gratin dish, pour over the sauce and then sprinkle over the cheese, if using. Return to the grill for 1–2 minutes until bubbling. Serve at once.

Serves 4–6

Preparation time: 15 minutes
Cooking time: 6–8 minutes

Cabbage, Beetroot and Apple Sauté

This is a favourite winter dish, especially at Christmas since the deep burgundy colour appears particularly festive. Buy the vacuum-sealed packets of beetroot cooked without the addition of vinegar.

- 40 g/1½ oz butter
- ½ red cabbage, thinly shredded
- 1 tablespoon chopped fresh thyme
- 2 teaspoons caraway seeds
- 1 teaspoon ground mixed spice
- 1 tablespoon sugar
- 150 ml/¼ pint red wine
- 2 tablespoons port
- 2 tablespoons red wine vinegar
- 2 dessert apples
- 250 g/8 oz cooked beetroot, cubed
- 50 g/2 oz pecan nuts, toasted
- salt and pepper

1 Melt 25 g/1 oz of the butter in a large frying pan and fry the cabbage, thyme, caraway seeds, spice and sugar for 10 minutes. Add the wine, port and vinegar and bring to the boil.

Cover the pan and cook over a low heat for 20 minutes.

2 Meanwhile, quarter, core and thickly slice the apples. Melt the remaining butter in a clean frying pan and fry the apples for 4–5 minutes until lightly golden. Add to the cabbage with the pan juices and the beetroot. Cover and cook for a further 15–20 minutes until the cabbage is tender. Season to taste. Stir in the nuts and serve at once.

Serves 4
Preparation time: 20 minutes
Cooking time: 55 minutes

Roasted Autumn Vegetables with a Garlic Sauce

Roasting vegetables in a hot oven draws out their natural sweetness and intense flavour. It is important to cut them into similar-sized pieces so they cook evenly.

- 1 large head garlic
- 2 large onions, cut into wedges
- 8 small carrots, quartered
- 8 small parsnips
- 12 small potatoes, halved if large
- 2 heads fennel, sliced thickly
- 4 rosemary sprigs
- 4 thyme sprigs

- 6 tablespoons extra virgin olive oil
- salt and pepper

GARLIC SAUCE:
- 1 large slice of day-old bread (about 75 g/3 oz)
- 4 tablespoons milk
- 75 ml/3 fl oz extra virgin olive oil

1 Blanch the whole head of garlic in boiling water for 5 minutes. Drain and pat dry on paper towels.
2 Put all the vegetables and herbs in a large roasting pan, placing the garlic in the middle. Season well and stir in the oil to coat the vegetables. Cover the pan with foil and place in a preheated oven, 220°C (425°F), Gas Mark 7, for 50 minutes. Remove the foil and bake for a further 30 minutes.
3 Remove the head of garlic. Carefully peel and discard the skin; mash the garlic flesh with a fork. Put the bread in a bowl, add the milk and soak for 5 minutes.
4 Place the bread and garlic flesh in a liquidizer and process to form a smooth paste. Gradually blend in the oil until evenly combined; season to taste.
5 Serve the roasted vegetables accompanied by the garlic sauce to dip.

Serves 4–6
Preparation time: 25 minutes
Cooking time: 1 hour 25 minutes
Oven temperature: 220°C (425°F), Gas Mark 7

VARIATION

Roasted Onions with Balsamic Vinegar

- 6 large red onions
- 3 tablespoons extra virgin olive oil
- 1 tablespoon chopped fresh thyme
- 1 tablespoon chopped fresh rosemary
- 2 garlic cloves, crushed
- 1 teaspoon coriander seeds, crushed
- 4 tablespoons balsamic vinegar
- 4 tablespoons red wine
- 1 tablespoon clear honey
- salt and pepper

1 Cut the onions into eighths from the stalk to the root without cutting all the way through and press open. Place in a roasting pan.
2 Combine the oil, herbs, garlic, coriander seeds and seasoning. Drizzle over the onions and place in a preheated oven, 220°C (425°F), Gas Mark 7, for 30 minutes.
3 Mix the vinegar, wine and honey together, pour a little over each onion and bake for a further 25–30 minutes until the onions are tender. Serve with the glazed juices.

Serves 6
Preparation time: 10 minutes
Cooking time: 1 hour
Oven temperature: 220°C (425°F), Gas Mark 7

Aubergine Towers

These stuffed aubergines sit up cheekily on the plate and are just too tempting to resist!

- 4 small aubergines – about 12 cm/ 5 inches long
- 2 tablespoons extra virgin olive oil, plus extra for brushing
- 1 small onion, chopped finely
- 2 garlic cloves, crushed
- 2 teaspoons grated lemon rind
- 1 teaspoon ground cumin
- ½ teaspoon ground cinnamon
- 40 g/1½ oz sultanas
- 40 g/1½ oz cashew nuts, toasted and chopped
- 2 teaspoons tahini paste
- 50 g/2 oz drained sun-dried tomatoes in oil, chopped
- 2 tablespoons chopped fresh coriander
- salt and pepper

TO SERVE:
- Fresh Tomato Sauce (see page 94) and Greek yogurt or Mushroom Gravy (see page 95)

1 Cut off the stem of each aubergine about 2.5 cm/1 inch from the top. Cut a slice from the bottom so that the aubergines will stand upright. Carefully scoop out the flesh, leaving the skin intact. Chop the flesh.
2 Heat the oil in a frying pan and fry the onion, garlic, lemon rind and spices for 5 minutes. Add the aubergine flesh and continue to cook for a further 6–8 minutes until tender. Stir in all the remaining ingredients and season to taste.

3 Spoon the filling mixture into the aubergines, brush with oil and arrange upright in a small roasting pan. Add about 1 cm/½ inch of boiling water and place in a preheated oven, 200°C (400°F), Gas Mark 6, for 40 minutes until cooked through. Serve at once with tomato sauce and Greek yogurt or mushroom gravy.

Serves 4
Preparation time: 25 minutes, plus making sauce or gravy
Cooking time: 55–60 minutes
Oven temperature: 200°C (400°F), Gas Mark 6

Mashed Potato with Coriander Root

Used extensively in Thai cooking, coriander root adds a delicate aromatic flavour to the mashed potato. The roots can be found, still attached to bunches of coriander, in some supermarkets or Asian food stores. Coriander stalks, chopped very finely, are a suitable alternative.

- 1 kg/2 lb floury potatoes, scrubbed
- 6 tablespoons extra virgin olive oil
- 5 g/¼ oz coriander roots, scrubbed
- 2 tablespoons chopped fresh coriander
- salt and pepper

1 Cook the potatoes in boiling, salted water for 15–20 minutes until tender. Drain well, then return to the pan and mash until smooth.
2 Meanwhile, heat the oil in a small pan, add the coriander roots and fry very gently until tender. Remove from the heat and stir in the chopped coriander. Transfer to a liquidizer and process to form a smooth paste.
3 Add the coriander paste to the mashed potatoes with plenty of salt and pepper and beat gently until evenly combined. Stir in a little milk to form a softer mixture, if wished, and serve at once.

Serves 4
Preparation time: 5 minutes
Cooking time: 15–20 minutes

Eggs and Cheese

Breakfast Gratin

4 tablespoons extra virgin olive oil

175 g/6 oz button mushrooms, quartered if large

1 onion, chopped roughly

4 small cooked potatoes, cubed

4 small tomatoes, halved

4 small eggs (size 5)

125 g/4 oz vegetarian Cheddar cheese, grated

2 tablespoons chopped fresh chives or parsley

salt and pepper

1 Heat half the oil in a large frying pan or skillet, add the mushrooms and onion and fry for 5 minutes until golden. Remove with a slotted spoon and set aside. Add the remaining oil and fry the potatoes for 5–6 minutes until golden.

2 Increase the heat, stir in the tomatoes and fry over a high heat for 2–3 minutes until lightly golden. Return the mushrooms and onions to the pan.

3 Make 4 holes in the mixture and carefully break an egg into each hole. Scatter over the cheese and place under a preheated hot grill for 4–5 minutes until the eggs are set and the cheese bubbling and golden.

4 Sprinkle over the chopped chives or parsley and serve at once.

Serves 4

Preparation time: 15 minutes

Cooking time: 18–20 minutes

Melanzane Parmigiana

This layered bake of aubergines and cheese is a classic Italian dish. The original version uses layers of mozzarella, but Cheddar gives a better texture and richer flavour.

- 6 aubergines
- salt
- 2 tablespoons extra virgin olive oil
- 1 quantity Fresh Tomato Sauce (see page 94)
- 250 g/8 oz vegetarian Cheddar cheese, grated
- 50 g/2 oz vegetarian Parmesan cheese, grated

1 Trim the aubergines and cut lengthways into thick slices. Sprinkle with salt and leave to drain in a colander for 30 minutes. Wash well, drain and pat dry on paper towels.
2 Brush the aubergine slices with oil and place on 2 large baking sheets. Roast the aubergines at the top of a preheated oven, 200°C (400°F), Gas Mark 6, for 10 minutes on each side until golden and tender.
3 Meanwhile, reheat the tomato sauce and keep warm.
4 Spoon a little of the tomato sauce into a lasagne dish and top with a layer of aubergines and some of the Cheddar cheese. Continue with the layers, finishing with the Cheddar. Sprinkle over the Parmesan cheese and bake for 30 minutes until the cheese is bubbling and golden.

Serves 6

Preparation time: 10 minutes, plus 30 minutes draining, plus making sauce
Cooking time: 50 minutes
Oven temperature: 200°C (400°F), Gas Mark 6

Eggs Benedict

This is a delicious variation of the classic recipe. Although there are several cooking stages to work through, each one is really quick and simple, particularly once you've mastered the art of making the perfect hollandaise sauce. For a special occasion, arrange the mushrooms in individual gratin dishes.

- 1 quantity Hollandaise Sauce (see page 94)
- 6 large cup mushrooms, stalks trimmed
- 6 tablespoons extra virgin olive oil
- 500 g/1 lb fresh spinach, trimmed
- 6 small eggs (size 4)
- cayenne pepper, to garnish

1 First make the hollandaise sauce. Place a piece of clingfilm over the surface of the sauce and sit the bowl over a pan of hot water to keep warm.
2 Arrange the mushrooms, cap side down, in an ovenproof dish. Drizzle over the olive oil, cover with foil and place in a preheated oven, 200°C (400°F), Gas Mark 6, for 20 minutes.
3 Meanwhile, wash the spinach and place in a large saucepan. Heat gently until just wilted. Drain, squeeze out the excess liquid and chop roughly. Poach the eggs in an egg poacher, or in a pan of gently simmering water, for 3–4 minutes until just cooked.
4 Remove the mushrooms from the oven, spoon the chopped spinach around the mushrooms and carefully place a poached egg on top of each mushroom.
5 Pour over the hollandaise sauce and place the dish under a preheated hot grill for 3–4 minutes until browned. Sprinkle with a little cayenne pepper and serve immediately.

Serves 6
Preparation time: 10 minutes, plus making sauce
Cooking time: 25–30 minutes
Oven temperature: 200°C (400°F), Gas Mark 6

Herb Roulade with Spinach and Ricotta

- 25 g/1 oz butter
- 40 g/1½ oz plain flour
- 1 teaspoon Dijon mustard
- 200 ml/7 fl oz semi-skimmed milk
- 50 g/2 oz vegetarian cheese, grated
- 4 eggs, separated
- 4 tablespoons chopped mixed fresh herbs (basil, chervil, chives, tarragon, thyme)
- salt and pepper

FILLING:
- 175 g/6 oz ricotta or curd cheese
- 2 tablespoons extra virgin olive oil, plus extra for oiling
- pinch of grated nutmeg
- 1 leek, chopped finely
- 500 g/1 lb frozen leaf spinach, thawed
- ¼ teaspoon freshly grated nutmeg
- Fresh Tomato Sauce (see page 94), to serve

1 Grease a 23 x 33 cm/9 x 13 inch Swiss roll tin and line with nonstick baking paper. Melt the butter in a saucepan, stir in the flour and mustard and cook over a low heat for 1 minute, then gradually add the milk, stirring until evenly blended. Bring the sauce slowly to the boil, stirring constantly until the sauce thickens. Cook over a low heat for 2 minutes.

2 Remove the pan from the heat, leave to cool slightly, then beat in the cheese, egg yolks, herbs and seasoning. Whisk the egg whites until stiff and fold into the sauce until evenly incorporated.

3 Pour the mixture into the prepared tin and place in a preheated oven, 200°C (400°F), Gas Mark 6, for 12–15 minutes until risen and firm to the touch. Remove from the oven and set aside to cool. Reduce the temperature to 190°C (375°F), Gas Mark 5.

4 Meanwhile, prepare the filling. Beat the cheese and half the oil together until smooth and season with nutmeg, salt and pepper.

5 Heat the remaining oil in a frying pan and fry the leek for 5 minutes. Drain the spinach well, squeeze out all the excess liquid and chop finely. Add to the leeks and cook gently for 5 minutes.

6 To assemble the roulade, turn out of the tin and carefully peel away the paper. Spread over the softened cheese and then the spinach mixture. Roll up from a short end and place on the oiled Swiss roll tin. Brush with oil and bake for 20–25 minutes. Serve hot, in slices, with fresh tomato sauce.

Serves 6
Preparation time: 40 minutes, plus making sauce
Cooking time: 40–50 minutes
Oven temperature: 200°C (400°F), Gas Mark 6, then 190°C (375°F), Gas Mark 5

Curried Parsnip and Cheese Soufflés

Don't be put off cooking soufflés because of their reputation for collapsing the moment they arrive at the table. As long as the taste is great, it doesn't really matter if they don't look perfect.

- 250 g/8 oz peeled parsnips, chopped
- 25 g/1 oz butter, plus extra for greasing
- 25 g/1 oz plain flour
- 2 teaspoons hot curry paste
- 200 ml/7 fl oz milk
- 40 g/1½ oz vegetarian Gruyère or Cheddar cheese, grated
- 3 eggs, separated
- 2 tablespoons chopped fresh coriander
- 40 g/1½ oz ground almonds, toasted
- salt and pepper

1 Steam the parsnips for 15–20 minutes until tender. Mash well and set aside to cool.

2 Melt the butter in a small saucepan, add the flour and cook for 1 minute, stirring. Stir in the curry paste and gradually add the milk, stirring constantly until smooth. Slowly bring to the boil, stirring constantly until thickened. Cook over a low heat for 2 minutes.

3 Remove the pan from the heat and stir in the grated cheese until melted. Cool slightly, then beat in the egg yolks with the cooled mashed parsnip, chopped coriander, half the toasted ground almonds and salt and pepper to taste.

4 Whisk the egg whites until stiff and carefully fold into the parsnip mixture until evenly incorporated.

5 Grease 6 large ramekin dishes and line with the remaining toasted ground almonds. Spoon in the soufflé mixture and place the ramekin dishes in a large roasting pan. Add enough boiling water to come two-thirds of the way up the sides of the ramekin dishes and place the roasting pan in a preheated oven, 200°C (400°F), Gas Mark 6, for 25 minutes until risen and golden. Serve the soufflés immediately.

Serves 6
Preparation time: 25 minutes
Cooking time: 45–50 minutes
Oven temperature: 200°C (400°F), Gas Mark 6

Basic Pancakes

This recipe is suitable for both savoury and sweet pancakes. They can be kept warm for up to 30 minutes: stack on a plate, cover with clingfilm and place over a pan of gently simmering water. They also freeze well, interleaved with greaseproof paper.

- 125 g/4 oz plain flour
- pinch of salt
- 1 egg, lightly beaten
- 300 ml/½ pint milk
- vegetable oil, for frying

1 Sift the flour and salt into a bowl and make a well in the centre. Gradually beat in the egg and then the milk to form a smooth batter with a thick pouring consistency. Cover and leave to rest for 20 minutes.
2 Using an omelette pan or small frying pan, about 18 cm/7 inches in diameter, brush the surface of the pan with a little oil and heat until just starting to smoke.
3 Take a ladleful of the batter, pour into the pan and quickly swirl the mixture to cover the base of the pan in a thin even layer. Cook for 2–3 minutes until set and browned underneath, then flip over with a palette knife and cook the other side for a further 1–2 minutes until browned. Remove from the pan and repeat with the remaining batter to make 8 pancakes, brushing the pan with a little oil before adding the next spoonful of batter.

Serves 4
Preparation time: 5 minutes, plus 20 minutes resting
Cooking time: 3–5 minutes per pancake

VARIATIONS

Spinach Pancakes

Drain 125 g/4 oz thawed frozen spinach and squeeze out excess liquid. Chop finely and beat into the batter with the milk.

Buckwheat Pancakes

Replace half the plain flour in the basic pancake mixture with an equal amount of buckwheat flour.

Herb Pancakes

Add 4 tablespoons chopped fresh herbs, such as mint, basil, parsley or tarragon, to the basic pancake batter.

Spinach Pancake and Asparagus Gratin

- 24 thick asparagus stalks
- 8 Spinach Pancakes (see left)
- vegetable oil, for oiling
- ½ quantity Classic White Sauce (see page 94)
- 50 g/2 oz vegetarian Cheshire cheese, grated

1 Trim the asparagus stalks and blanch in a large pan of lightly salted, boiling water for 2 minutes. Drain, refresh under cold water and pat dry on paper towels.

2 Place 3 asparagus stalks on each pancake and roll up. Place the pancakes seam-side down in an oiled baking dish.

3 Pour over the white sauce and scatter over the cheese. Place under a preheated medium-hot grill and cook for 8–10 minutes until bubbling and golden. Serve at once.

Serves 4

Preparation time: 5 minutes, plus making pancakes and sauce
Cooking time: 12–15 minutes

Puddings and Desserts

Rhubarb, Apple and Double Ginger Crumble

125 g/4 oz plain flour

50 g/2 oz ginger biscuits, crushed or ground in a food processor

25 g/1 oz porridge oats

100 g/3½ oz unsalted butter, plus extra for greasing

3 tablespoons light muscovado sugar

500 g/1 lb rhubarb, chopped

2 tablespoons chopped preserved stem ginger,

plus 2 tablespoons ginger syrup from jar

50 g/2 oz caster sugar

4 tablespoons water

375 g/12 oz dessert apples, peeled, cored and sliced

1 Sift the flour into a bowl and stir in the ground ginger biscuits and oats. Rub in the butter until the mixture resembles breadcrumbs, then stir in the muscovado sugar.
2 Place the rhubarb in a saucepan with the chopped ginger, ginger syrup, caster sugar and water. Heat gently, cover and simmer for 10 minutes.
3 Place the sliced apples in a greased pie dish. Add the rhubarb mixture and sprinkle over the crumble topping. Place in a preheated oven, 190°C (375°F), Gas Mark 5, for 40 minutes until the filling is bubbling and the topping is golden. Serve hot.

Serves 8
Preparation time: 20 minutes
Cooking time: 50 minutes
Oven temperature: 190°C (375°F), Gas Mark 5

Baked Lemon and Bay Custards

This recipe is a variation of the old classic lemon tart. Here, the lemon custard is infused with bay leaves, giving it a heady scent. The custard is baked in a very low oven: if the oven is too hot the custard will curdle. Check after 40 minutes – the centres should be almost set but still move a little – they will firm up as they cool.

- 12 bay leaves, bruised
- 2 tablespoons lemon rind
- 150 ml/¼ pint double cream
- 4 eggs
- 1 egg yolk
- 150 g/5 oz caster sugar
- 100 ml/3½ fl oz lemon juice

1 Put the bay leaves, lemon rind and cream in a small saucepan and heat gently until it reaches boiling point. Remove from the heat and set aside for 2 hours to infuse.
2 Whisk the eggs, egg yolk and sugar together until the mixture is pale and creamy and then whisk in the lemon juice. Strain the cream mixture through a fine sieve into the egg mixture and stir until combined.
3 Pour the custard into 8 individual ramekin dishes and place on a baking sheet. Bake in a preheated oven,

120°C (250°F), Gas Mark ½, for 50 minutes or until the custards are almost set in the middle. Leave until cold and chill until required. Return to room temperature before serving.

Serves 8
Preparation time: 5 minutes, plus 2 hours infusing
Cooking time: 55–60 minutes
Oven temperature: 120°C (250°F), Gas Mark ½

Poached Figs in Cassis with Cinnamon Sauce

Fresh figs can be disappointingly lacking in flavour. The best figs are those enjoyed straight from the tree. However, this method of poaching them in a blackcurrant liqueur and red wine will add flavour to the fruit.

- 300 ml/½ pint red wine
- 150 ml/¼ pint cassis
- 2 cinnamon sticks
- 2 strips lemon peel
- 2 strips orange peel
- 300 ml/½ pint water
- 12 large firm ripe figs, washed

SAUCE:
- 150 g/5 oz Greek yogurt
- 2 tablespoons Greek honey
- 1 teaspoon ground cinnamon

1 Place the wine, cassis, cinnamon sticks, citrus peel and water in a saucepan and bring to the boil.
2 Add the figs, cover the pan and simmer gently for 10 minutes until the figs are just tender. Do not over-cook or the figs will fall apart.
3 Remove the figs with a slotted spoon and place in a serving dish. Bring the poaching liquid to a rolling boil and simmer until it is reduced by half and is thick and syrupy. Pour over the figs and leave to cool.
5 Meanwhile, combine all the sauce ingredients together and set aside to allow the flavours to develop. Serve the figs at room temperature with the cinnamon sauce.

Serves 4
Preparation time: 10 minutes, plus chilling
Cooking time: 10 minutes

VARIATION

Poached Pears

Replace the 12 figs from the main recipe with 4 firm, ripe pears. Peel the pears and simmer them in the syrup for about 40 minutes until cooked through but not mushy. Remove the pears from the syrup and continue as left.

Pear and Cardamom Flan

- 175 g/6 oz plain flour
- ¼ teaspoon salt
- 100 g/3½ oz unsalted butter, diced, plus extra for greasing
- 2 tablespoons caster sugar
- 1 egg yolk
- 1 teaspoon caster sugar, to serve (optional)

FILLING:

- 125 g/4 oz unsalted butter, softened
- 75 g/3 oz caster sugar
- 2 small eggs (size 4), lightly beaten
- 75 g/3 oz ground hazelnuts
- 25 g/1 oz ground rice
- seeds from 2 cardamom pods, crushed
- 1 teaspoon grated lemon zest
- 4 tablespoons soured cream
- 3 small firm pears

1 Sift the flour and salt into a bowl and rub in the butter until the mixture resembles fine breadcrumbs. Stir in the sugar and gradually work in the egg yolk and 1–2 tablespoons cold water to form a soft dough. Knead lightly, wrap in cling film and chill for 30 minutes.

2 Roll out the pastry on a lightly floured surface and use to line a greased 23 cm/9 inch fluted flan tin. Prick the base and chill for a further 20 minutes.

3 Line the pastry case with nonstick baking paper and baking beans and place in a preheated oven, 220°C (425°F), Gas Mark 7, for 10 minutes. Remove the paper and beans and

bake for a further 10–12 minutes until the pastry is crisp and golden. Reduce the temperature to 180°C (350°F), Gas Mark 4.

4 In a bowl beat together the butter and sugar until pale and light and then gradually beat in the eggs, a little at a time until incorporated. Lightly beat in all the remaining ingredients, except the pears. Pour the mixture into the prepared pastry case.

5 Peel and halve the pears and scoop out the cores. Thinly slice each pear lengthways. Be careful not to change the shape of the pears. Then, using a palette knife, carefully transfer the sliced pears to the pastry case, arranging them neatly on the filling. Bake the flan for 55–60 minutes until golden and firm in the middle. Serve the flan warm, sprinkled all over with a little caster sugar and some whipped cream, if liked.

Serves 6
Preparation time: 20 minutes, plus chilling
Cooking time: 1 hour
Oven temperature: 220°C (425°F), Gas Mark 7, then 180°C (350°F), Gas Mark 4

Peach, Apricot and Blueberry Gratin

This quick and simple dessert is best made when fresh apricots and peaches are in season. American blueberries are available most of the year, or raspberries make a good substitute.

- 4 firm ripe peaches, halved, stoned and sliced very thinly
- 6 firm ripe apricots, halved, stoned and sliced very thinly
- 175 g/6 oz blueberries
- 250 g/8 oz mascarpone cheese
- 250 g/8 oz Greek yogurt
- 3 tablespoons light muscovado sugar
- 1 teaspoon ground cinnamon

1 Spoon the peaches, apricots and blueberries into a gratin dish.
2 Beat the mascarpone and yogurt together and spread over the fruit.
3 Combine the sugar and cinnamon, sprinkle over the gratin to cover the surface and cook under a preheated hot grill for 5–6 minutes until the sugar is caramelized. Leave to cool for a few minutes before serving.

Serves 6
Preparation time: 10 minutes
Cooking time: 5–6 minutes

VARIATION

Amaretti Fruit Gratin

Crumble 125 g/4 oz amaretti biscuits in the bottom of the gratin dish, press down into the dish and then add the fruit and 4 tablespoons Kirsch and cook as described in the main recipe.

Stocks and Sauces

Vegetable Stock

- 4 tablespoons sunflower oil
- 2 whole garlic cloves
- 2 onions, chopped roughly
- 2 leeks, sliced
- 4 carrots, chopped
- 2 potatoes, diced
- 4 celery sticks, sliced
- 4 ripe tomatoes, chopped roughly
- 125 g/4 oz mushrooms, wiped
- 125 g/4 oz rice
- 1 bouquet garni (see page 8)
- 1.75 litres/3 pints water

1 Heat the oil in a pan, add the garlic, onions and leeks and fry gently for 10 minutes. Add the carrots, potatoes and celery and fry for a further 10 minutes. Add the remaining ingredients, bring to the boil, cover and simmer for 30 minutes.
2 Strain through a fine sieve and use as required.

Makes 1.5 litres/2½ pints
Preparation time: 15 minutes
Cooking time: 40 minutes

Fresh Tomato Sauce

- 1 kg/2 lb ripe tomatoes, chopped roughly
- 2 tablespoons extra virgin olive oil
- 2 garlic cloves, chopped
- 2 tablespoons chopped fresh basil
- 1 teaspoon grated lemon rind
- pinch of sugar
- salt and pepper

1 Place all the ingredients in a saucepan and bring to the boil. Cover and simmer gently for 30 minutes.
2 Remove the lid and simmer for 20 minutes until the sauce is thick. Taste and adjust the seasoning.

Makes about 600 ml/1 pint
Preparation time: 10 minutes
Cooking time: 50 minutes

VARIATION

Quick Tomato Sauce

Use 2 x 425 g/14 oz cans chopped tomatoes. Cook as above, but simmer for 10 minutes only.

Classic White Sauce

- 600 ml/1 pint milk
- 1 small onion, chopped roughly
- 1 bay leaf
- 50 g/2 oz butter
- 50 g/2 oz plain flour
- salt and pepper

1 Put the milk, onion and bay leaf in a pan and heat until just boiling. Remove from the heat, set aside for 20 minutes. Strain and set aside.
2 Melt the butter in a pan, stir in the flour and cook over a low heat for 1 minute. Remove from the heat and beat in the milk a little at a time until blended. Return to a low heat and stir constantly until thickened. Bring to a gentle boil, stirring; simmer for 2 minutes. Season with salt and pepper.

Makes about 600 ml/1 pint
Preparation time: 25 minutes
Cooking time: 8–10 minutes

VARIATION

Classic Cheese Sauce

Add 125 g/4 oz grated Cheddar or Gruyère cheese to the cooked sauce off the heat.

Hollandaise Sauce

- 2 egg yolks
- pinch of sugar
- ¼ teaspoon salt
- 1 tablespoon white wine vinegar
- 1 tablespoon water
- 1 teaspoon Dijon mustard
- 125 g/4 oz unsalted butter, diced
- white pepper

1 Place the first 6 ingredients in a bowl and whisk until frothy.

2 Set the bowl over a pan of gently simmering water and continue to whisk until the whisk leaves a trail.
3 Remove from the heat and whisk in the butter a little at a time, beating after each addition, until thickened. The sauce should be frothy and of a pouring consistency. Taste and adjust the seasoning and serve at once.

Makes about 200 ml/7 fl oz
Preparation time: 5 minutes
Cooking time: 5 minutes

Mushroom Gravy

- 15 g/½ oz dried ceps
- 25 g/1 oz butter
- 4 shallots, chopped
- 500 g/1 lb field mushrooms, sliced
- 2 tablespoons plain flour
- 150 ml/¼ pint dry sherry or white wine
- 4 thyme sprigs
- 4 rosemary sprigs
- 600 ml/1 pint Vegetable Stock (see left)
- salt and pepper

1 Soak the ceps in 300 ml/½ pint boiling water for 30 minutes. Drain, reserving the liquid. Slice the ceps.
2 Melt the butter in a pan and fry the shallots for 5 minutes. Add the mushrooms and ceps and fry for a further 5 minutes until tender.
3 Stir in the flour, cook for 1 minute. Gradually whisk in the sherry or wine and cep liquid and boil for 5 minutes. Strain through a sieve into a clean pan.
4 Add the herbs and stock, and boil for 10–15 minutes until reduced by half. Season, strain and serve at once.

Makes about 400 ml/14 fl oz
Preparation time: 10 minutes, plus making stock and soaking
Cooking time: 20 minutes

Onion & Wine Gravy

- 50 g/2 oz butter
- 2 large onions, chopped roughly
- 150 ml/¼ pint red wine
- 4 tablespoons port
- 600 ml/1 pint Vegetable Stock (see left)
- 1 bay leaf
- 2 rosemary sprigs, bruised

1 Melt 15 g/½ oz of the butter in a pan, add the onions and cook over a low heat for 10 minutes. Add the wine and port and boil for 3 minutes. Add the stock, bay leaf and rosemary and simmer, covered, for 20 minutes.
2 Strain into a clean pan; boil until reduced to 300 ml/½ pint. Whisk in the remaining butter a little at a time until thickened slightly and glossy.

Makes 300 ml/½ pint
Preparation time: 10 minutes, plus making stock
Cooking time: 45 minutes

French Dressing

- 1 tablespoon white or red wine vinegar
- 1 teaspoon Dijon mustard
- pinch of sugar
- 6 tablespoons extra virgin olive oil
- salt and pepper

Put the vinegar, mustard, sugar and salt and pepper into a small bowl and whisk well. Gradually whisk in the oil until well blended.

Makes about 100 ml/3½ fl oz

VARIATION
Balsamic Dressing

Whisk together 2 teaspoons balsamic vinegar, 2 teaspoons wholegrain mustard, salt and pepper and then gradually whisk in 5 tablespoons extra virgin olive oil.

Pesto Sauce

- 1 garlic clove, crushed
- 25 g/1 oz pine nuts
- 25 g/1 oz basil leaves
- 75 ml/3 fl oz extra virgin olive oil
- 2 tablespoons grated vegetarian Parmesan cheese
- salt and pepper

1 Place the garlic, pine nuts and basil in a liquidizer and process until fairly smooth. Gradually beat in the oil, then stir in the cheese, taste and adjust the seasoning.

Makes about 150 ml/¼ pint
Preparation time: 10 minutes

VARIATION
Red Pesto

Add 50 g/2 oz drained and sliced sun-dried tomatoes in oil to the above ingredients and blend roughly.

Photographer:
Gus Filgate
Home Economist:
Louise Pickford
Jacket Photographers:
Philip Webb
Ian Wallace
Jacket Home Economists:
Fran Warde
Louise Pickford